UNOFFICIAL

MINECRAFT STEMLAB FOR KIDS

Family-Friendly Projects for Exploring Concepts in Science, Technology, Engineering, and Math

QUARRY

JOHN MILLER AND
CHRIS FORNELL SCOTT

Brimming with creative inspiration, how-to projects, and useful information to enrich your everyday life, Quarto Knows is a favorite destination for those pursuing their interests and passions. Visit our site and dig deeper with our books into your area of interest: Quarto Creates, Quarto Cooks, Quarto Homes, Quarto Lives, Quarto Drives, Quarto Explores, Quarto Gifts, or Quarto Kids.

Inspiring | Educating | Creating | Entertaining

© 2018 Quarto Publishing Group USA Inc.

First Published in 2018 by Quarry Books, an imprint of The Quarto Group, 100 Cummings Center, Suite 265-D, Beverly, MA 01915, USA. T (978) 282-9590 F (978) 283-2742 QuartoKnows.com

Quarry Books titles are also available at discount for retail, wholesale, promotional, and bulk purchase. For details, contact the Special Sales Manager by email at specialsales@quarto.com or by mail at The Quarto Group, Attn: Special Sales Manager, 401 Second Avenue North, Suite 310, Minneapolis, MN 55401, USA.

10 9 8 7 6 5 4 3 2 1

ISBN: 978-1-63159-694-0
Digital edition published in 2018
Library of Congress Cataloging-in-Publication Data available

Design: Kathie Alexander
Page Layout: Kathie Alexander
Photography: John Miller and Chris Fornell Scott
Illustration: Annie Scott

NOT AN OFFICIAL MINECRAFT PRODUCT. NOT APPROVED BY OR ASSOCIATED WITH MOJANG.

Printed in China

MIX
Paper from responsible sources
FSC® C016973

To my mother,
who has resolutely supported my every effort
in life and continues to be my biggest fan.
Thank you for inspiring me every day.

—JM

To my first group of students,
who showed me the power of learning through
Minecraft at Santa Ynez School, and to all
the kids at Minecrafter Camps.

—CFS

ACKNOWLEDGMENTS

Simply put, we could not have written this book without the extensive support and enthusiasm of our wives, family, and friends, who have encouraged us throughout the process. They've willingly put up with weeks of project clutter, photo shoots, and lost weekends, and we cannot thank them enough.

Special thanks to Annie Scott for sketching the sketchnote challenges.

We'd also like to acknowledge the creative magic and thoughtful guidance that Joy Aquilino and the wonderfully talented people at Quarto Publishing have provided us.

And you, our reader, who makes this all worth it: thank you for spending your time reading our books.

Contents

Introduction:
Notes for Parents and Teachers

Welcome to the second in our series of Minecraft Lab books. We are thrilled that you've chosen to add our latest book to your library. The overall theme of this book is connecting STEM—concepts in science, technology, engineering, and math—with Minecraft play. If you've read our first book, *Unofficial Minecraft Lab for Kids*, the format will be familiar. There are six themed quests, each of which presents four labs. Each of the labs has two parts: an out-of-game/family activity that requires hands-on exploration; and an in-game building and crafting activity.

Since *Unofficial Minecraft Lab for Kids* was published, we've learned that there are lots of folks just like us, looking to incorporate their kids' interests into family activities. Minecraft has become an invaluable way for families all over the world to play together constructively.

More than ever, parents and teachers are looking for unique and engaging ways to connect a child's interests with learning objectives. Using the quests and labs, we've found that Minecraft is one of the best ways to connect those objectives with kids' innate curiosity. While many games are focused on beating a score or another team, Minecraft's open-ended nature encourages and enhances teamwork. According to feedback and examples we've received from our readers, both kids and parents have loved working through the labs in our first book.

WHY STEM?
STEM is much more than in-school assignments and labs. It's about being curious and asking questions. Ultimately, STEM is about testing ideas, thinking about real-world problems, and developing solu-

Minecraft builds by readers of *Unofficial Minecraft Lab for Kids*: Elliott Coffey, age 7 *(far left)*; Charlotte and Claire Scott; and Teagan Carter *(far right)*.

tions that improve lives and advance the world. What STEM education for elementary and middle-school kids typically lacks is a pathway to real-world problems. Minecraft can serve as an access point.

Minecraft offers a perfect blend of urgency and abundance within an immersive world that pulls players deeper into the game. Players can quickly build solutions to problems, tear down, and rebuild.

With a computer or smartphone and an internet connection, it's easier than ever to find immediate answers to questions. But what about the questions that can't be answered or that haven't been asked? For those, we need individual thinking, creativity, and minds that are free to explore the possibilities.

Through the labs in *Unofficial Minecraft STEM Lab for Kids*, which connect real life with in-game play and encourage Minecraft

players to ask themselves why they designed, built, or changed something, new possibilities in Minecraft can be discovered.

HOW TO USE THIS BOOK

Unofficial Minecraft STEM Lab for Kids is for parents, caregivers, and educators—any adult who wants to connect the Minecraft player(s) in their life with STEM learning. It's intended to help bridge the gap between game-play and engaging STEM concepts.

The best way to use this book is to work through the labs with your Minecraft playing partner. The labs are intended to develop thinking skills and communication. Feel free to skip around from lab to lab, or to start at the beginning and work through the labs consecutively. We encourage you to extend and modify the labs to reflect your interests and those of your Minecraft player(s).

SKETCHNOTING: INCORPORATING VISUAL THINKING

Throughout this book, players are encouraged to keep a science field journal in which they keep track of their findings, recording everything they observe and collect, much as a scientist working in the field would. By journaling their observations, your players will be able to keep track of their findings. When scientists jot down all their observations, they free space in their brain's working memory to focus on other areas during their research. Not all observations have clear connections while journaling, which is why scientists jot down as much as possible.

We offer some examples of field journal entries below and on the opposite page to inspire your players, who can either follow our examples or make up their own. Note that ours are a mix of writing and drawing often called *sketchnoting* or visual journaling. By combining visuals with text, we find it's easier to jot down ideas more quickly.

Most field journals typically include the time of day, weather, location, plants and/or animals observed, soil, measurements, etc. Our sketchnotes also include drawings, diagrams, and questions—lots of questions.

Here are a few basic guidelines to share with your player:

- Just jot down ideas. Don't worry about how they look. No one is grading this work. The journal is only for your player's own scientific experiments.
- Highlight important items by making them darker or bolder with a pencil, pen, or marker.
- Doodle, add your personality, and have fun!

Sample sketchnotes for Lab 23 (left) and Lab 19 (right).

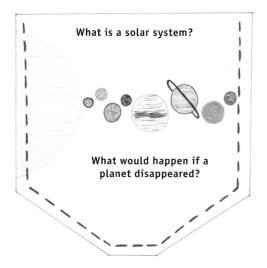

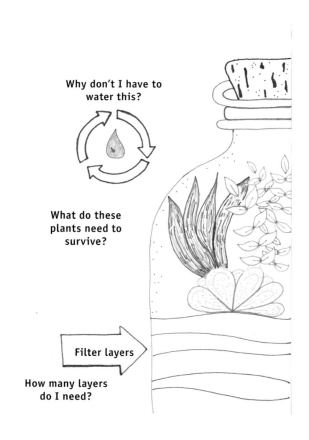

Sample sketchnotes (from top)
for Labs 15, 9, and 5.

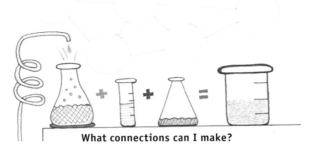

What connections can I make?

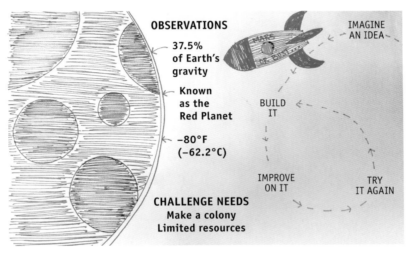

OBSERVATIONS

37.5%
of Earth's
gravity

Known
as the
Red Planet

−80°F
(−62.2°C)

IMAGINE
AN IDEA

BUILD
IT

TRY
IT AGAIN

IMPROVE
ON IT

CHALLENGE NEEDS
Make a colony
Limited resources

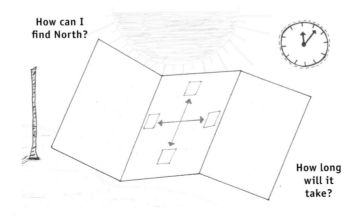

**How can I
find North?**

**How long
will it
take?**

What Is Minecraft?

When players enter a newly created Minecraft world, they often experience a sense of awe and wonder as they move through a place that has been uniquely generated just for them. They find themselves walking through a jungle or across a deserted beach or scaling a tall mountain to get a better view. They might encounter a vast sandy desert or a deep red and brown mesa. Through their travels, they may see wild horses, cute little rabbits, or other exotic beasts as each day passes.

At its core, Minecraft is a simple game. A novice can get a general feel in minutes for how the game is played, despite the fact that no instructions come with it. You can play by yourself or with others, and the game can be played across multiple devices, from computers to smartphones and tablets to gaming consoles.

It's also deceivingly detailed, as advanced players can attest. Mining is pretty straightforward. After acquiring wood or stone, players create a pickaxe following a simple recipe and then start digging. But what to do with all that material? Using recipes, players craft new and varied resources and items that can, in turn, be used to craft even more useful items.

As the game has continued to develop, more items and recipes are introduced with each new version. New animals and monsters, called mobs, become available, as do new blocks, including speciality blocks that directly support learning on a high level. Minecraft has also evolved from a simple game into a rich learning platform. There is even an education edition of the game that is available for schools, supported by lesson ideas and custom worlds available for download.

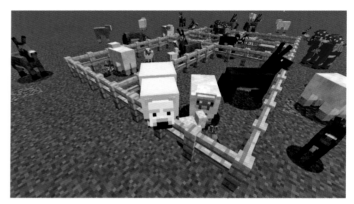

Would you like to build your own zoo in Minecraft? There are plenty of animals to choose from.

The game has been used to generate elaborate stories where players go on quests, fight monsters, and solve riddles. It has spawned hundreds of books and encouraged a generation of kids to become writers and storytellers.

Minecraft is being used by budding game developers to create games within the game and to teach the next generation of coders valuable skills and concepts. With players numbering in the millions, there is a huge demand for people who can manage servers, create rich content, and design and build ever more elaborate worlds that will push the limits of the game to new levels.

How to Play

Everyone who plays Minecraft needs to have purchased a license. Licenses are awarded for purchasing the game, either through the website Minecraft.net or through an app store for the Pocket Edition and console versions. The license is tied to your log-in credentials, which means you need to sign in to play each time. There are multiple versions of the game written for specific devices.

After launching the game, you have a choice between single player, multiplayer, and in some cases, Minecraft Realms. A realm is a subscription-based miniserver where players can invite their friends across the globe to play together in a shared world. Players will not notice a difference in how the game looks and feels between single and multiplayer.

As it implies, single player is a solitary experience. You are the only player in a vast, unlimited world. It is often used by players as a practice area, a place they can use to hone their skills on their own terms and without interruption. After choosing single player, you have the option to open an existing world or create a new one.

If you elect to create a new world, you have the further option to choose either survival or creative mode (above right) and you have the opportunity to give the world a name. The game will now generate a world for you and when finished, you'll find yourself in it.

In multiplayer mode, players most often collaborate and share resources toward the common good. Teamwork is usually emphasized, and building or otherwise developing resources is a large-scale affair.

To play with others, someone has to open up a game to be played over a network. It can be someone sitting in the same room as you, in which case it is referred to as a LAN, or local area network, or you can meet up with friends on a public Minecraft server. With either option, you will need to know the address of the server you wish to join. If you don't see any options for games to join, click on Direct Connect and type in the address of the server. If you are joining a local network, ask the person that started the game to share the address or invite you to join. The player that starts the game gets to choose the game conditions.

Survival Mode and Creative Mode

When beginning a new game, there are two common game mode options players must choose between. In survival mode, players begin with nothing and find themselves in a randomly generated and unique world to explore. The Sun is up and it's time to get busy cutting down trees and building a shelter. About 10 minutes later, when night falls, monsters like zombies, skeletons, and the explosive creeper come out of hiding and will attack players out in the open.

Build a shelter quickly in survival mode. As night falls, monsters come out!

Players who survive the first night return to work as a lumberjack or miner while acquiring valuable resources such as wood, stone, coal, and iron. While safely in their shelters at night, players craft tools, armor, and weapons and eat food harvested during the day to replenish their health. Food is acquired by killing animals or by farming crops. With each passing day, players become stronger and can eventually venture out at night and fight off the monsters trying to kill them.

With creative play, every player has access to an unlimited supply of all the blocks, tools, and mechanisms available in the game. Monsters will not attack, and players stay healthy and do not require food. Blocks can be placed or destroyed with one click and everyone can fly. This high degree of freedom allows players to work through the design process and teach themselves and each other how to build ever more elaborate structures and mechanisms. It encourages communication, experimentation, testing hypotheses, and sharing knowledge. This mode is often used to create carefully crafted and expansive adventures for players to experience in survival mode.

Cycle through each tab to see all of the blocks available in creative mode.

Getting to Know the Controls

Moving around in Minecraft requires the use of both hands. In the case of the Pocket Edition and console versions, your thumbs play an important role. If you are playing on a computer, you will be using the W, A, S, and D keys and either a mouse or a trackpad capable of clicking left and right.

Upon entering a game, move your mouse or your finger on the trackpad, left and right. Your character's head will respond by moving left and right. Press and hold W and your character will move forward in the direction you are facing. Press A and your character slides to the right; press D and they will slide to the left. Pressing S moves your character backward. When you come upon an elevated block in front of you, tap the spacebar *and* W and your character will hop atop it.

When you come upon a common block, such as dirt or a tree, hold down the left mouse or trackpad button and your character will "punch" the object. Hold the button down until the object shrinks in size and floats in front of you. Press W and move forward to collect it.

Right-click to swing your pickaxe, open a door, fight off a monster, or place blocks. When you destroy blocks and pick them up, they appear in your inventory, partially visible as slots on the bottom of your screen. You can access each slot by cycling through the number 1 through 9 on your keyboard. Highlight the block you wish to place and it appears in your character's right hand. Now find a location where you wish to place the block and right-click. The block will appear in the center of the crosshairs on your screen. Blocks can be placed only within five blocks of where you are standing.

BLOCKS THAT SUPPORT DEEP LEARNING WITH STEM

There are multiple blocks and gadgets in Minecraft that directly and indirectly support STEM learning. You'll be introduced to many of them in the very first lab and uncover more secrets in each lab, thereafter. You'll make use of these items for structural elements in buildings, as apparatus to conduct experiments, and to compare their properties to their real-world counterparts.

Redstone

Redstone is a source of power in Minecraft. You can think of it as electricity. It takes on many forms. It can be found in its natural state as redstone ore, deep underground. It's a fairly common block to discover in survival mode and is easy to identify because red sparks dance off the stone.

Three states of redstone (from left to right): ore found underground, dust obtained from smelting ore, and a block of redstone crafted from nine piles of dust.

As a power source, redstone can be turned on and off using one of several switches: lever, button, trip wire, or pressure plate. Players use redstone dust to create circuits on the ground that connect switches to mechanisms.

Switches allow players to control the flow of power to mechanisms along each circuit.

Power Sources

In addition to switches, there are five common sources of stored power in Minecraft:

- **Daylight sensors** monitor the light source and supply power to connected circuits when night falls.
- **Observer blocks** are placed adjacent to another block, such as a piston, and monitor it for changes. If a change is detected, the observer block emits power down the circuit to a mechanism.
- **Redstone torches** look like a regular torch except they glow a soft red. The glowing red torch is a power source and when placed next to a circuit or mechanism, it will supply power to it.
- **Redstone blocks** are power sources with special features. For one, they are a constant source of power and cannot be turned off. They can also be moved by pistons and work underwater.
- A **trapped chest** supplies power to a circuit or other mechanism when opened (activated).

Redstone power sources (from left to right): daylight sensor, observer block, redstone torch, redstone block, and trapped chest.

Transmitters

Power is transmitted through redstone dust, which makes circuits. But dust can transmit power over a distance of only 15 blocks before the power fades to nothing. Repeaters are used to extend the signal. Repeaters also contain a mechanism that allows the player to slow down the transmission of the signal. Comparators compare states of blocks along the circuit and can adjust signal strength.

Power travels through and can be controlled by repeaters, redstone dust, and comparators.

Mechanisms

What to do with an unlimited supply of power? Build elaborate infrastructure, such as lighting systems, rail stations, automated doors and traps, and advanced devices such as printers and calculators. Players can attach multiple types of mechanisms to their circuits and power them on and off, as needed. Several of the most popular mechanisms are

- **Pistons** react to a completed circuit by pushing a block in the direction the piston is facing. A regular piston can push up to 12 blocks in a line. A sticky piston can both push and pull blocks that are stuck to the green and gooey piston head.

- **Command blocks** are very powerful blocks not found in the standard inventory; they can execute commands on the Minecraft server, changing the game for players. They are activated by redstone and are capable of doing things such as changing the game mode, giving players one or more items, summoning monsters, or teleporting players to different locations.
- The opening and closing of **fence gates**, **trapdoors**, and **conventional doors** can be automated with redstone by attaching a switch. Wooden gates and doors don't require a switch, but iron doors need power to operate.
- **Droppers** are blocks that push or eject items inside outward. They can also push an item into a container, like a chest next to them. Droppers can even be placed adjacent to each other to move an item over a long chain or pipe.
- **Redstone lamps** provide a large amount of light when activated. They are very popular for making monster traps. Monsters spawn in the dark, but they can then be attacked by surprise when the lamp is turned on.
- **Note blocks** play notes when activated. They mimic the sounds made by instruments such as guitars, flutes, bass drums, and pianos. Players can tune their way through several octaves.
- **Hoppers** are handy to have when mining. They are used to automate the transfer of items from one container to another. Items dropped or sucked into the top of the hopper will wind up neatly stacked into a chest.
- **Dispensers** are similar to droppers in that they distribute items to players in an orderly manner. Loaded dispensers push items out the front when activated, but items like arrows, eggs, and snowballs are shot out like the projectiles they are.

Redstone-activated mechanisms include (from left to right) pistons, command block, fence gate, door, trapdoor, dropper, redstone lamp, note block, hopper, and dispenser.

RAIL

One of the most enjoyable activities in Minecraft is to hop aboard a minecart and take a journey over rails. Rails are most often used to transport miners and materials underground. In large cities, they are used as aboveground and underground railroads as well as spectacular roller coasters that push the limits of physics.

There are powered rails and unpowdered rails. Powered rails contain their own redstone power source, so minecarts flow freely over powered rails if they are activated. Powered rails that are not activated will act as a brake. Unpowered rails do not contain a power source, but unlike powered rails, they can bend, which allows carts to change direction.

Detector rails are used to check the contents of a minecart that passes over them. Depending on how full the cart is, the detector rail may activate other redstone mechanisms along the rail line.

Finally, powered activator rails are used to activate properties of blocks that are contained in the minecart. For example, if a minecart contains a block of TNT and passes over an activator rail, the rail will light the fuse, causing an explosion shortly thereafter.

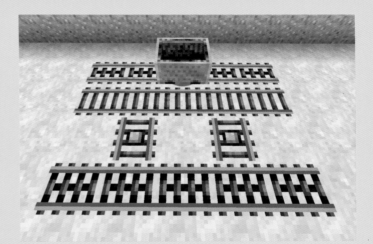

Minecart rails (from back to front): powered rails, unpowered rails, detector rails, and activator rails.

THE MINECRAFT SKILL SET

It should come as no surprise that educators are using Minecraft to support learning across the curriculum and at all grade levels. What might surprise parents and nongamers is how this game has inspired young and old, alike, to forge careers and reinvent themselves as content producers and creators, designers, professional builders, server managers, and YouTube personalities.

It seems Minecraft has spawned not just a generation of players but also a community of highly creative and innovative practitioners. Everyone that plays this game comes away with a sense of wonder at the experience and generally can't wait to return to dig, build, and craft. But is there actual learning going on while playing this game and does it transfer to real-life skills?

Researchers and educators that have experience with Minecraft often point to a set of complex skills that players experience and encounter while engage in game play. These include

- **Analytical skills:** Players see or anticipate a problem and can visualize and articulate it to others. Maybe there is a mob spawner in the next room, and you have to figure out how to shut it down. Or, perhaps, you want to build an automated fireworks show using redstone.
- **Critical thinking:** Players take the facts they have gathered and make decisions. This is especially important when designing sophisticated mechanisms. Minecraft is a safe place to make mistakes through trial and error and to work through testing a hypothesis.
- **Problem solving and creative thinking:** This is the most broadly employable and demanded skill. A day does not go by in Minecraft without players reacting to a problem they face, be it in creatively designing a building or in performing a needs analysis to determine crafting priorities.

- **Communication:** Communication from the onset of any project is critical, whether it is among peers or between service providers and clients. Multiplayer Minecraft games are immensely popular and designing and building these massive worlds involves dozens of people, including many specialists. Effective communication strategies are critical throughout the process.
- **Soft skills:** These refer to character traits that enable us to get along with each other. Players are often asked to be patient, express empathy, and monitor self-control during the game. Cooperative teamwork and a strong work ethic are expected for builds to be successful.

For this book, we've asked five of our friends to help us take a deeper look at what Minecraft teaches us and how this skill set translates into personal growth and employable skills. Each is an expert in his or her field and has a vast range of experiences and backgrounds (see pages 17-21).

A FINAL WORD

It's our hope that the adults who use this book will have an open mind and be an active participant in each of our labs. You'll share what we've discovered by playing alongside our students and children. Minecraft provides a family-friendly immersive experience. It is collaborative and encourages creative problem solving and rewards logical thinking, deduction, and patient problem solving. Effective communication is key to its success. It's a game, but it's also a training ground for the next generation of business leaders, entrepreneurs, scientists, and great thinkers.

Sign up for our Minecraft newsletter on our website Minecraftercamp.com. Our newsletter will help you stay informed with the latest ideas and strategies to help your child continue to learn STEM and, of course, Minecraft.

Beth Bates: @Sqaishey

www.youtube.com/user/sqaishey

Beth, aka Sqaishey Quack, is a YouTube star who produces a series of videos that tell stories about her character's exploits. Sqaishey Quack is a creative little yellow duck that loves going on challenging adventures. The videos she creates are filmed in a let's play format where viewers follow the story through the eyes of her character. Although this may sound like an easy task, producing videos of the consistently high quality that Beth releases merges a film director's skill set with that of a technical editor, writer, and performance artist.

Using Minecraft to tell stories is wildly popular because it is so creatively flexible. Beth says, "Because Minecraft is a very open world game, your imagination is your only boundary; this makes telling your own story really easy and fun."

Beth also runs a Minecraft server called Quacktopia and is keenly aware of her responsibilities and expectations of visitors to the server. Players each receive an area where they can creatively build whatever they want. "This server is special to me," she explains. "It allows loads of players to come together in a safe environment and play."

The server has also really opened her eyes to the power of community. When she started, she had no idea how popular it would be, but "it quickly became a place where loads of people worked together and created amazing things!" She visits the server regularly and is thrilled to find so many kids telling jokes and working together to create incredible things.

Beth shares that each new player who joins receives an auto-welcome message and "everyone on the server welcomes the new member to our community, giving them advice on how to make their own plot or inviting them to theirs to help build something." Beth is inspired by the collective imagination of kids, a valuable life lesson for all of us.

Stephen Reid: @ImmersiveMind

www.immersiveminds.com

Stephen is director of Immersive Minds, a creative content producer in learning and teaching. He blends engaging technologies with solid teaching foundations to support education and soft-skills development. Although he uses Minecraft extensively in his profession, he also delves into other technologies, such as 3D printing, TinkerCAD, SketchFab, and virtual reality.

Among his specialties is engaging students in deeply philosophical subjects, such as the refugee crisis, religious and moral education, and debates on ethics and values. He develops Minecraft maps with this purpose in mind and works as a consultant in the global Minecraft community, sharing experiences with kids, parents, universities, charities, and businesses.

His projects focus on using Minecraft to develop the whole learner. He designs activities to develop analytical, critical, and creative thinking skills and asks learners to engage in the world around them, find problems they might be able to solve, and create solutions within a Minecraft world; he then challenges them to apply it to the real world.

He elaborates, "Often this involves children exploring environmental science; making outdoor trips to visit sites to rivers, dams, wind farms, coal plants, etc.; running tests and gathering data that will inform their builds; and then returning to create solutions in Minecraft. To this end, we have had fish ladders designed for dams in Scotland, offshore wind farm models for Europe, river pollution models that show how different land use such as farming can affect rivers in Asia, working coal mines, and more."

Stephen is most impressed by each child's ability to reach beyond his expectations and deliver "a portfolio of knowledge and understanding on any subject." He provides an example where students developed a WWI trench map "in which students recreated the trenches of the Somme, then immediately began to tell stories of the soldiers in those trenches. Sound effects began, stories started, study continued, and soon we had a letter-writing session that has now become a finished lesson for all. The students just couldn't stop developing the learning around this map."

Stephen likes to consistently blend the real world with Minecraft by having students visit sites before re-creating them in the game, writing letters from the perspective of the people involved in the event they are documenting, and reading and becoming inspired by books about the subject. He stresses that it is hugely important to create a balance between digital and analog learning, as well as building skills in, and beyond, school.

Garrett Zimmer: @pbjellygames
www.minegage.com

Garrett works with Minecraft as a game-based learning tool. He trains and supports adults interested in designing serious game lessons with Minecraft and works with young players to develop peer-to-peer learning games. He views Minecraft as a game, a tool, and a game-design engine.

He says, "It's my theory and experience that when students take a curriculum or lesson they need to learn and begin to design a peer-learning game to play together, they are engaged in levels of higher-order thinking that goes beyond a traditional pedagogy, become far more engaged, and invest far more energy in their learning. The outcomes of this are vast and exciting, as students, parents, and educators are creating games that are designed for synchronous learning and enjoyment."

Garrett describes a recent workshop experience where a group of parents and children worked through a lesson design model and came up with a scenario-based adventure game that would address common childhood safety issues, such as looking both ways before crossing the street. He states, "In the end, the group collectively prepared a game design that was both memorable in the game play itself, was a communication-heavy process, and created some unique moments of critical thought and meta cognition for the kids and parents during the design process. With the final challenge to create the game, kids and parents were deeply engaged together."

Elizabethan London courtesy of MineGage Studios.

Garrett emphasizes that one of Minecraft's strengths, and one reason why it is so successful, is its ability to appeal to a variety of gamer types. Players who like to design and build in creative mode and express themselves artistically, partake of adventure in survival mode, design games for others to play, or participate in competitive battles all interact in a broad community to help the game evolve. He has discovered that Minecraft has helped him grow as a designer and communicator, which, in turn, helps him work with and engage others outside the game.

Adam Clarke: @thecommonpeople
www.thecommonpeople.tv

Adam Clarke, aka Wizard Keen, is a storyteller, an artist, and a producer. He describes how he treats Minecraft as "digital clay: something that can be made and then remixed and made into something different time and again." He designs and creates collaborative and creative experiences for players to engage with.

He loves a challenge, particularly one that requires creative thinking. With Templecraft (*https://goo.gl/sCN9f9*), Adam was one of the producers that created a Minecraft version of artist David Best's "Temple" work in Derry, Northern Ireland. A giant wooden temple was constructed and then open for seven days; 60,000 people visited over the next week and left remembrances behind. At the end of the week, the temple was purposely burned down.

Adam set about creating a build similar to Best's real-world temple, a place "where Minecraft players of all ages could come together, leave messages, symbolic objects and mementos in the same act of letting go of the past, honoring the lost, and letting in the future."

Creating something serious and emotional within Minecraft was the challenge. In a short amount of time, he assembled a wonderful team of builders and they went about the task of putting the temple together and getting it ready for the public. Visitors to the Minecraft server left behind remembrances and tributes to their loved ones and, just as the actual temple was burned, the Minecraft temple was set ablaze.

Many of Adam's projects begin life as collaborations with his wife, Victoria Bennett. He says the most important part of any project is "the point where we sit down at the kitchen table, spread out a huge sheet of paper, and start brainstorming. This way of working has been invaluable and that planning and research enriches the Minecraft design process."

When we asked Adam why games like Minecraft are so popular. "They feel authentic and real," he said. "They are places where our kids are in charge." With so many kids playing this game, he is especially excited about the future, where "we can see their narrative skills flourish and expand into playful collaborations, mini games, and communication that is global and inclusive."

Visitors were encouraged to let go of the past and honor the lost in Templecraft. Courtesy of Adam Clarke, Digital Producer.

Johan Kruger: @dragnoz

www.dragnoz.com

Johan, aka Dragnoz, describes himself as a designer of interactive experiences that tap into players' preexisting knowledge about Minecraft. He is the behind-the-scenes architect of several very popular Minecraft maps and series, including *We Are the Rangers* and *Wonder Quest*. Johan stresses how developing Minecraft worlds is far more than just placing blocks. He says, "Minecraft is a platform that has redefined what self-directed learning is."

He fully engages his analytical, creative, and problem-solving skills with each iteration of a map. In the *Wonder Quest* series (*https://goo.gl/Nf2Yef*), he found his hands and mind fully engaged, stating how especially challenging it was in "working with builders to create the sets, working with producers to ensure what they aim to achieve is actually doable in Minecraft, working with the actors to help them understand the new mechanics and features, and then executing and creating everything from fully functioning ecosystems to working rain cycles."

For the conservation-themed *We Are the Rangers* (wearetherangers.com), he had to create the atmospheric mood of being on an African plain by changing sensory aspects of the game without using traditional "mods." The result is a seamless and highly effective learning experience.

Johan is a master of Minecraft's in-game coding language. As you complete several of the labs in this book, you will be exposed to this attribute that allows players to massively modify game mechanics and is often the first experience young players will have writing code. Johan enjoys hearing from gamers who became coders after being inspired by his work and the work of others.

In his view, Minecraft skills seamlessly blend into the real world. He uses programming and logical thinking the most, but focuses in on a third: "I think the biggest takeaway skill is problem solving. Whether you build massive buildings or sit in a hole in the ground trying to survive the night, you are constantly problem solving."

Dragnoz is a master of special effects in Minecraft.

QUEST 1

Pistons, Rails, and Redstone

To complete this quest, Minecrafters and their families will get an opportunity to work with several of the most advanced blocks in Minecraft.

LAB 1

REDSTONE LABORATORY
Craft a redstone science laboratory with field stations and a solar telescope.

LAB 2

ALL ABOARD
Build a Minecraft railroad and marble roller coaster.

LAB 3

GRAVITY IMPACT
Test and measure the effects gravity has on falling objects.

LAB 4

PISTON POWER
Create doors, traps, and secret entrances to protect your home, while learning the power of fluids.

Are you a fan of fun science shows that test out crazy ideas? In the first in-game activity for this book, you'll set up your own redstone-powered science laboratory where you'll run experiments and use as a hub for future labs. The lab will feature redstone mechanisms and solar sensors to automate doors, turn lights on and off, play notes when someone visits, and notify you when it's safe to go outside.

In the hands-on activity, you'll construct a solar telescope that can be used to safely make observations of the surface of the Sun.

■ **APPROXIMATE TIME TO COMPLETE**
30 minutes

■ **MATERIALS**
Multipurpose tape
Cardboard box with lid
White paper
Scissors
Pen
Sewing needle

 STAY SAFE!
Never look directly at the Sun. See "What's the Science?" for details.

Family Activity: Solar Telescope

The Sun provides us not only with light, but with energy as well. In this activity, you'll build a solar telescope that will safely allow you to look at the Sun's reflection.

1. Using the multipurpose tape, cover all sources of light inside the box and lid. Tape the sheet of white paper to the inside of the box at one end. (fig. 1).

2. Place the lid on the box. Identify a location about one-third of the way down from the end opposite the paper. Draw an egg-shaped outline that approximates the width of your face. Next, cut around the outline you drew (fig. 2). You'll place your forehead through this hole, so make sure it's wide enough. To ensure that as little light as possible enters the box, apply tape around the edges of the hole.

3. Place the lid tightly on the box. In the box end opposite the paper, push the needle through the box and/or the tape and pull it out the other side. The cleaner the hole you create, the sharper the image will be (fig. 3).

5. Your solar telescope is complete. With the lid firmly in place, point the pinhole in the direction of the Sun and place your eyes through the opening in the lid. (fig. 4).

Fig. 1: Tape a white sheet of paper inside one end of the box.

Fig. 2: Cut out a hole wide enough to see through.

Fig. 3: Plunge the needle through the box end opposite the white paper.

Fig. 4: Point the pinhole end toward the sun. Look inside to see the sun's image reflecting off the white paper.

WHAT'S THE SCIENCE?

By allowing a tight beam of light to enter the box, which produces a remarkably sharp and accurate image of the Sun, a solar telescope allows us to look at the Sun safely. **It's NEVER safe to look directly at the Sun** because its light and energy are intensified by the cells of our retinas, at the backs of our eyes. Those cells are very sensitive to light and help us see things when light levels are low. Looking directly at the Sun can burn and even destroy this very important part of our eyes.

Start your Minecraft STEM journey by building a crazy science laboratory and installing at least three mechanisms:

1. Daylight sensors to turn the lights on when it gets dark and to play a sound to notify you when the Sun is coming up.

2. A doorbell that will play a lovely tune when your guests arrive.

3. Piston tables to set your lab equipment on.

■ **GAME MODE**

Creative

■ **APPROXIMATE TIME TO COMPLETE**

2+ hours

SKETCHNOTE CHALLENGE

Create a map of your new world. First, sketch out the layout for your laboratory and determine where your equipment will go. Next, use arrows to connect your lab (hub) to at least four different field stations, each located in a different biome. Don't forget to name your field stations.

1. **Create a new Minecraft world in creative mode to use for exploring the labs in this book. Find a location with access to an ocean or a river and that has some flat space and several biomes nearby. Locate a spot for your laboratory. Sketch a blueprint for your building in your field notebook.**

2. **Level out an area to build upon and construct your lab, keeping these guidelines in mind:**

   • **Scientists need clean, open space to work in.**

   • **Scientists spend a lot of time making observations, so include windows.**

   • **You'll need a flat roof with access (stairs) from below. Make sure your roof is at least 2 blocks thick (fig. 1).**

3. **First, let's set up a daylight sensor and two note blocks in a series. At first light, the sensor will signal the note blocks to play two notes to notify the hardworking scientists that it's daytime. On your roof, set up your materials in the following order: daylight sensor, redstone dust, note block sitting on top of a gold block, a repeater, and then another note block sitting on top of a gold block (fig. 2).**

Fig. 1: Provide lots of open space and include a staircase to access the roof.

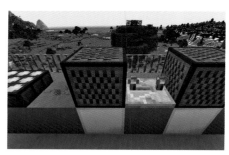

Fig. 2: This setup will let you know when the Sun comes up each day by playing a short tune.

Fig. 3: Test two different "not gate" setups to see how they work.

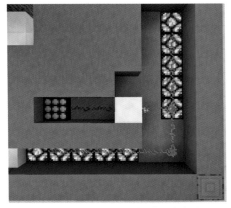

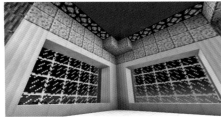

Fig. 4: This is what your automatic lighting should look like from the top of the roof (above) and from underneath it.

4. Right-click on each note block and you will hear a pleasant chime. Additional right-clicks will adjust the pitch of each note. Place the repeater in line with the note blocks. Adjust the signal delay by right-clicking the redstone torch on the repeater 1, 2, or 3 times. You can add more repeaters to delay the note even longer. In figure 2, the circuit is active and the repeater is set to maximum delay.
Tip: You can use a switch in place of the sensor to test your system. When it sounds perfect, replace the switch with the sensor and wait for the Sun to rise.

5. Next, you'll attach a sensor to a "not gate," which will produce a signal when the sensor is not active at nightfall. In other words, the not gate will turn the lights on at dusk and will keep them on until the Sun rises.

6. As an experiment, set up a simple not gate between a sensor and a redstone lamp in the following order: daylight sensor, redstone dust, an opaque block like quartz with a redstone torch attached on the opposite side away from the sensor, more redstone dust, and then the redstone lamp (fig. 3).

7. You can now re create this sequence on your roof. In our example (fig. 4), we've connected 10 redstone lamps to one daylight sensor and one not gate. Determine where you want to place your lamps and personalize your automated lighting system.

(continued)

8. To make a musical note doorbell, you'll need a switch, note blocks, redstone dust, and repeaters. Place the note blocks on top of blocks of your choice to re-create different instruments. Visit *https://goo.gl/P6ew06* to see a selection of instruments you can choose from. Redstone dust may be placed only on a flat surface, or it can run down a block like a staircase. Note blocks will work only if there is a block of air above them, so you will need to dig a pit at least three blocks deep in front of and below your doorbell (fig. 5). When placing repeaters, the stationary redstone torch should be placed opposite the switch in the direction the signal is traveling (fig. 6). You can cover up the surface of the pit when finished, but make sure each note block has an air block above it and there are no blocks directly on top of your redstone wiring.

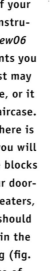

NOW TRY THIS

For players seeking more of a challenge:

- After learning more about pistons and trapdoors in Lab 4, add a secret entrance to your lab.
- Create more elaborate tunes for your note block doorbell.
- Build an observatory building on top of your roof.

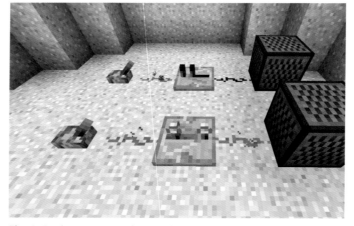

Fig. 5: You need to connect three note blocks together with repeaters between them for your doorbell. Make sure there is a block of air above each.

Fig. 6: In the top setup, the note block will not work because the redstone torch on the repeater faces toward the lever. In the bottom setup, the torch correctly faces toward the note block.

FIND IT ONLINE

- Australian YouTuber Flabaliki has created a series of very popular short videos that will teach you the basics about using redstone. Find the playlist here: *https://goo.gl/rrJydV*
- Check out this video from UnspeakableGaming that explores deep learning through redstone: *https://goo.gl/x007op*

Fig. 7: Place a redstone torch beneath a piston to extend it and use it as a table.

Fig. 8: What kinds of things do you think a laboratory should contain? Here are a few ideas.

9. You'll need lots of workspace inside your laboratory. Place several pistons around your lab and activate each by placing a redstone torch beneath them (fig. 7). You can use regular or sticky pistons for tables. *Tip:* Place slabs around the pistons to create a slightly elevated floor. Your new tables will now be at the perfect height.

10. Your laboratory is mostly complete, so now it is time to add some finishing touches. What kinds of equipment do scientists need in a laboratory? We've included brewing stands, a furnace, lab tables, a fish tank, and windows the color of a rainbow. We decorated our lab with item frames containing blocks like ores, plants, items found in rivers and oceans, and a bunch of redstone (fig. 8). What did we miss?

GO BEYOND

Redstone mechanisms, power sources, and transmitters can be combined in a seemingly infinite number of ways by very imaginative creators. Challenge yourself throughout this book to go beyond and design contraptions that test scientific concepts like computing, robotics, engineering, and physics.

All Aboard

Welcome aboard! In this lab, you'll build a railroad to transport visitors and supplies throughout your realm. You'll learn how to automate much of your system, and create a mini Grand Central Station near your laboratory. Out-of-game, you'll build a giant marble roller coaster that tests the boundaries of physics!

FIND IT ONLINE

- You'll love watching this marble roller coaster that students built in their school cafeteria: https://goo.gl/hgX7E6

■ APPROXIMATE TIME TO COMPLETE
1–2 hours

■ MATERIALS
³⁄₄-inch (2 cm)-wide flexible foam tubing, enough to complete your design
Scissors
Multipurpose or masking tape
Assorted props such as books, pots, cardboard tubes, and plastic cups to elevate your rail
Marbles
Graph paper to sketch your design (optional)

Family Activity: Make a Roller Coaster

This requires a real team effort and keen design and engineering skills, so gather as many family and friends as you can.

1. Flexible foam tubing usually comes preslit down the length of one side. Run the scissors carefully along the seam to open it completely, then turn it 180 degrees and cut the split tubing lengthwise until it separates into two equal pieces. Connect each section of tubing at the underside only. Adding tape to the top of the rail may impede the marble (fig. 1).

2. Your coaster should begin at a high point but, ultimately, make its way to the ground. Along the way it can speed up, slow down, and even change direction. Experiment by adding supports and fun features like bridges, curves, and tunnels (fig. 2).

3. You can take better advantage of limited space by designing several changes of direction in your coaster. Test out designs to see which one best switches the marble from one track to another (fig. 3).

4. You'll likely need plenty of tape. If running along a wall, be sure to use wall-safe tape. Our patio table was the perfect spot (fig. 4).

Fig. 1: Tape rails together on the underside only.

Fig. 2: Add loops, curves, bridges, and tunnels.

Fig. 3: A switch in direction enables the marble to better use limited space.

Fig. 4: After final assembly, give it a go!

WHAT'S THE SCIENCE?

It's all about energy. Everything has stored energy called *potential energy*. The marble is waiting for a push to release its energy. The energy it releases is called *kinetic energy*, sometimes referred to as *movement energy*, which can be transformed into other kinds of energy used by humans to power up.

Your challenge is to make a rail system that will begin at your science lab and take you, or your cargo, on a beautiful tour of each biome's unique animals, plants, and scenery. You may want your system to take riders in a loop, beginning and ending at your lab, or you may want to allow for travelers to hop on and off at two or more stations.

- **GAME MODE**
  Creative

- **APPROXIMATE TIME TO COMPLETE**
  2 hours

- **PLATFORMS**
  Normal rails
  Powered rails (increases minecart speed if powered with redstone)
  One or more note blocks
  Buttons, levers, and trip wire
  Minecarts
  Detector rails (activates a redstone mechanism when a minecart passes over it)
  Redstone dust and redstone torches
  A command block (issues commands to the server)
  One dispenser filled with minecarts

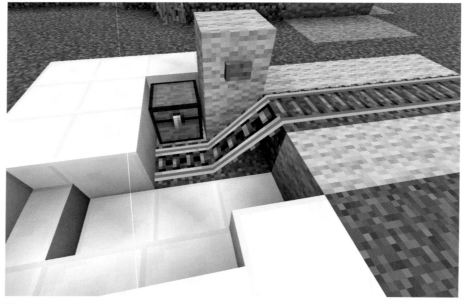

Fig. 1: Construct a one-way station everywhere you think visitors may want to explore.

1. Create a single-stop station by digging a hole 1 block deep and 2 blocks wide. Place two powered rails inside the hole and connect one end with normal rails. Place any block of your choice on ground level, adjacent to the pit. Place a button on the block facing the powered rails (fig. 1). Finally, place a minecart on one of the powered rails, push the button, and off you go! Connect each station to your system.

Fig. 2: A two-way station looks like the letter T. Place a lever at the intersection so players can select a travel direction.

Fig. 3: When this minecart rolls over a detector rail, it activates a note block to alert you that a minecart is coming.

2. A two-way station is handy when you want to allow riders the option of choosing a direction to travel. Follow the directions in step 1 to create a one-way station, but you'll also need to place a lever within reach at the intersection of the rail line (fig. 2). Before pushing the button to go, riders will pull the lever to set the direction of travel.

3. Detector rails activate (supply power to) mechanisms like note blocks, redstone lamps, and command blocks. Place one detector rail in your line and run redstone dust from it to a mechanism of your choice. When the cart rolls on top of it, the mechanism is activated (fig. 3).

(continued)

SKETCHNOTE CHALLENGE

It's sometimes easier to understand something as complicated as redstone by sketching a diagram. In this challenge, sketch a rail line that includes each type of rail and mechanism. Label each part and use colors inspired by the actual devices.

Fig. 4: The end of the line. Program a command block to teleport you out of the cart and to your doorstep.

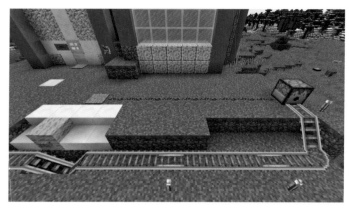

Fig. 5: This setup summons a minecart when you step on a pressure plate. The waypoint stops the cart to allow you to hop aboard.

4. Use a detector rail and a command block to automatically teleport you to your front door when your journey ends. Set it up like the example in step 3, but replace the note block with a command block. You can get a command block by typing

   /give @p minecraft:command_block

   A command block will pop into your inventory. Walk over to the front door of your lab and press F3 on your computer. Look for XYZ followed by three numbers. Those identify your exact location. Write them down.

5. Place and connect your command block with redstone dust to the detector rail. Right-click on the command block and in the box type in the following, replacing XYZ with your coordinates. Leave a space between each coordinate:

   /tp @p x y z

   Click DONE.

6. Test it out by hopping into a minecart and riding over the detector rail. You should be transported to your front door. We didn't want a bunch of empty minecarts lying around, so we added a lava pit at the end of the line (fig. 4).

7. Call a minecart to your front door by connecting a pressure plate to a dispenser filled with minecarts. Connect the dispenser to your rail line using powered rails and normal rails. The powered rails need a redstone lamp next to them or below them to activate. We added a waypoint in the line so that the cart stops in front of the lab (fig. 5).

Fig. 6: Add a trip wire to switch rail directions.

Fig. 7: Run redstone dust between the trip wire and the junction. When activated, the junction will switch the direction of travel temporarily.

8. Use a trip wire to automatically switch rail direction. Carts with cargo will go one way and riders will go another. Connect the trip wire between two blocks that are at least 3 blocks apart. Both trip wire mechanisms need to be 2 blocks high with the rail between them (fig. 6). With wire in your hand, right-click on the mechanism to attach.

9. Working on the other side of the mechanism, connect the right trip wire to the rail that is at the junction of your two lines. In our example, riders will travel left and cargo will continue ahead (fig. 7). Test your system. As players activate the trip wire, the redstone will engage and switch them to the left track. Minecarts with cargo will slip under the trip wire and continue straight ahead.

NOW TRY THIS

Activator rails switch or (activate) items inside a minecart, such as hoppers or TNT. Try activating and deactivating hoppers along one of your lines. Send a minecart with TNT across an activator rail and inside a mountain for some explosive fun.

GO BEYOND

Is a zigzag rail line slower than one built over a straight line? Test it out by building two lines that cover the same distance (blocks) and time each. Which one is faster?

In this lab, you'll test gravity in and out of game. In-game, you'll measure and test the effect gravity has on objects; in the family activity, you'll measure Earth's gravity by observing the impact of items landing in a soft substance.

Record the impact of several items dropped onto a bed of flour.

■ **APPROXIMATE TIME TO COMPLETE**
30 minutes

■ **MATERIALS**
Scoop
Flour
Tray
Ruler
Data table for recording your results
4 or 5 objects of different sizes and
weights, like rocks, marbles, and a
bouncy ball

1. Scoop about 3 cups (360 g) of flour onto your tray. (Note: The flour will dust the surrounding surface as you conduct your experiment!) Use the scoop to smooth out the flour base. Measure and record the depth of the flour base (fig. 1).

2. Drop one item at a time. Measure the depth and diameter of the crater from each impact, then smooth out the flour to prepare for the next object (fig. 2).

3. Log your findings in your science journal. Use a table like the one shown opposite, top, to keep track of them. Jot down other observations to record as much as possible during the experiment (fig. 3).

Family Activity: Testing the Effects of Gravity

OBJECT	SIZE OF OBJECT	CRATER DEPTH	CRATER DIAMETER	OTHER OBSERVATIONS
Large bouncy ball	6 inches (15 cm)	1 inch (2.5 cm)	4 inches (10 cm)	The large, yellow bouncy ball hit the flour surface and then bounced off and onto the floor.
Rock	2 inches (5 cm)	1¼ inches (3.2 cm)	2¾ inches (7 cm)	The rock made a larger cloud of flour than the bouncy ball.
Building-block toy	1 inch (2.5 cm)	1 inch (2.5 cm)	1½ inches (4 cm)	The flour got stuck inside the holes of the building block toy.

Fig. 1: Spread the flour in a baking pan. Create a smooth surface to make it easy to measure the impacts.

FIND IT ONLINE

Here's a great video that demonstrates Galileo's theory of gravity: *https://goo.gl/mXojgZ*

Fig. 2: Use a ruler to measure the depth of the crater or the depth of the flour left at the bottom of crater. Measure the diameter of the impact, as well.

Fig. 3: Record the size of the object, impact crater, and any other observations in your science journal.

WHAT'S THE SCIENCE?

Greek philosopher Aristotle was the first to try to describe gravity. He theorized that a 100 kg weight would fall twice as fast as a 50 kg weight. According to legend, Italian scientist Galileo tested this theory by dropping objects from the Leaning Tower of Pisa and found that the force of Earth's gravity is constant.

Allowing gravity to pull items onto the tray of flour resembles the impact of meteors hitting planets and moons. Look through a telescope or use an online resource to see the effects of meteors and comets on the Moon, Mars, and Earth because they were attracted by their force of gravity.

Every Minecrafter knows there's something strange about in-game gravity. Falling block items like sand, gravel, and concrete powder are subject to its force, but when stones and trees are mined, they mysteriously defy it. In this activity, you'll test the effect of gravity in Minecraft. Experiment by activating a redstone lamp with different inputs, including dropped items, tower height, redstone signal length, and type of redstone block. Keep track of your data, just as you did in the family activity.

■ **GAME MODE**
Creative

■ **APPROXIMATE TIME TO COMPLETE**
45 minutes

1. **Build a tower of blocks to measure distance more easily. Colored wool works great for the tower. We alternated between yellow and black wool (fig. 1).**

2. **Place a wooden pressure plate at the base of the tower. Connect the pressure plate with one piece of redstone dust to any redstone-activated block, like a piston or lamp (fig. 2).**

Fig. 1: Build the tower by interchanging color blocks. The different colors will help you measure the speed it takes the object to fall.

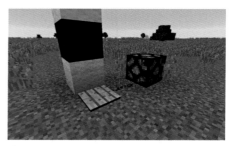

Fig. 2: Place a pressure plate at the base of your measurement tower. Start by connecting with just one piece of redstone dust to activate your redstone lamp.

Fig. 3: To build a redstone ladder, you need to start with a tower of blocks. Start your 2 × 10 vertical wall 2 blocks to the left of your measurement tower.

3. **To help make the drops consistent, build an automatic dropping mechanism. Start by building a 2 × 10 block vertical wall 2 blocks to the left of your colored block tower. The wall will allow you to add slabs that will hold the redstone dust (fig. 3).**

4. Place the stone slabs on the 2 × 10 wall in an offset pattern. Make sure the lowest slab is an inverted slab; it shouldn't be touching the ground. Place your first slab on the top half of your lower-left block wall (fig. 4).

5. Add redstone dust on top of each slab. Place a piston facing toward the measurement tower on the top slab. At the base of the ladder, place redstone on the ground and a redstone repeater to boost the redstone signal (fig. 5).

6. Compare gravel, sand, concrete powder, and the anvil using your simple remote-drop mechanism. Change the distance from your pressure plate to the redstone lamp. Adjust the height of your simple drop mechanism. Switch your pressure plate with different types of pressure plates. Do the blocks fall at different speeds? What happens to the blocks when they drop (fig. 6)?

Fig. 4: This redstone ladder uses quartz slabs. Start the first slab by placing it at the top half of your lowest block in the wall.

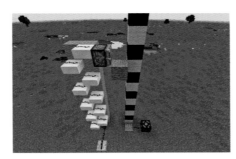

Fig. 5: Place redstone dust on top of each slab. There are different types of redstone ladders; try your hand at designing a different version.

Fig. 6: Flip your lever to activate the piston. The piston pushes a block to fall along the wall.

SKETCHNOTE CHALLENGE
Sketch your experiment. What did you experience that you didn't expect? How high can you build an automatic dropper tower?

NOW TRY THIS

- Does gravity affect objects differently if they're tied together? What if they were loosely tied together? Craft a wireless redstone contraption using a command block and the /setblock command.

- Build a vacuum chamber to demonstrate the force of gravity without air resistance.

- Galileo didn't just drop items off the Leaning Tower of Pisa (see page 37), he also tested with an inclined plane, like a ramp. Try crafting ramps in and out-of-game to test speeds.

- Try the Anti-Gravity Star-Miner mod available for the Java edition of Minecraft.

Piston Power

Most commonly found inside an internal combustion engine, pistons move up and down and turn a shaft that eventually propels a vehicle. The key benefit of a hydraulic piston is the mechanical advantage—the amount of force—gained by using it, since pressure within the system can't be lost. (See "What's the Science?" for more information.)

In the hands-on activity, build a piston using simple household materials. In-game, explore piston traps to protect your home from pesky mobs.

WHAT'S THE SCIENCE?

Scientist Blaise Pascal (1623–1662) discovered the law of fluid pressure, also known as Pascal's principle, when the pressure applied to one side of a closed system containing fluid and pistons is transferred to the other side of the system undiminished because the pressure within the system is equal. We can change the mechanical advantage by changing the size of the system and the distance the fluid travels.

Create a hydraulic piston with a balloon, baggie, and a hose, then test it to see how much it can lift. Does it require more, less, or the same amount of force to lift the objects?

■ **APPROXIMATE TIME TO COMPLETE**
   30 minutes

■ **MATERIALS**
   Small tubing or hose
      (we used aquarium air line tubing)
   1 plastic zippered snack baggie
   Water
   1 balloon
   Packing tape
   2 empty plastic containers
   A selection of small objects

1. Gather up your supplies to make your own hydraulic piston. If you don't have a balloon, you can substitute a zippered baggie (fig. 1). If you're using a balloon, blow into it to soften it up, to allow for easier movement of the water.

2. Slip one end of the tubing through the zippered opening in the baggie. Slip the other end into the balloon. Make sure the tubing extends far down into both the balloon and the baggie (fig. 2).

Fig. 1: Gather your materials.

Fig. 3: Check for leaks in the hydraulic system before you press on the baggie.

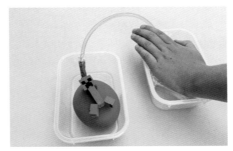
Fig. 4: Press on the baggie to watch the balloon fill with water and lift up the item. It's funny to put a creeper on a balloon full of water because creepers and water don't mix.

Fig. 2: Insert the tubing far into both the balloon and the baggie. Tape the balloon closed, first, before filling the baggie with water.

3. Seal the balloon with tape first, then fill the baggie with water, zip it closed, and seal it well with tape. Place the balloon and baggie in separate plastic containers, which can act as supports for larger items like books and rocks, then test the seal on the baggie by pressing down on it (fig. 3). Water will pour out of a poorly sealed baggie. If needed, refill the baggie with water and fix the seal before continuing to the next step.

4. Start with a light object on top of the balloon. Slowly press down on the plastic baggie full of water and watch as the balloon fills with water and lifts the item (fig. 4). Start with something light, then try heavier objects like books or rocks to see how much your hydraulic piston can lift.

The piston appears to be a simple block that just pushes and pulls things, but it really can be used for much more. Hydraulic pistons don't exist in Minecraft; rather, pistons use the mysterious electrical power from redstone. In this activity, we build a few variations of redstone piston contraptions, including a Jeb trap.

■ **GAME MODE**
Creative

■ **APPROXIMATE TIME TO COMPLETE**
1 hour

SKETCHNOTE CHALLENGE
Sketch the Jeb trap in your science journal. Design your house around the Jeb trap.

FIND IT ONLINE
- Check out Mumbo Jumbo's video on five simple piston traps and doors: *https://goo.gl/F1Xx5w*

Fig. 1: Dig out the area according to the image. Place the lowest horizontal sticky piston in front of the sand blocks.

1. Build a 4 × 9-wide pit 3 blocks deep. One block in from the sides, place 8 horizontal sticky pistons that will retract to pull the middle parts back. Check the image for the clever blocks around the bottom that will hold redstone and the sticky pistons (fig. 1).

2. Place 4 sticky pistons pointing vertically next to the lower horizontal pistons. These pistons will hold blocks that look like the ground. Place redstone repeaters behind the upper horizontal sticky pistons. Drop redstone dust around the edges to connect all the pistons (fig. 2).

3. The Jeb trap is now complete and ready to be activated. We used prismarine blocks to make the floor more obvious during the build. Switch out the prismarine for grass blocks for a truly incognito trap (fig. 3).

4. With the Jeb trap deactivated, dig down several block layers to add lava or water at the bottom to capture creepers, zombies, and other hostile mobs.

5. Find a regular-looking hill or mountain for the super secret simple fortress. Dig out an interior and design the inside of your new cave.

6. Place two horizontal sticky pistons in the entrance to your mountain cave. Use the same block found in the mountain to stick on the end of the sticky piston. When the piston is deactivated, the piston retracts and reveals a simple two-block door (fig. 4).

7. Place a lever on the block next to the sticky pistons. Use your stealth skills to hide the lever. Place a temporary block in front of the lever to effectively hide it (fig. 5).

NOW TRY THIS

- How much can your hydraulic piston lift? What can you do to make it lift ten times as much?
- How might you apply your knowledge of pistons from this lab for use in the Chain Reaction Contraption (see Lab 22)?
- Where else could you use a Jeb trap? How would it work if it were mounted vertically?

Fig. 2: This is the most complicated part of the Jeb-trap build. Take your time. The trap will work, just follow what you see in the images. If it doesn't work, check your redstone connections. You may need to add a repeater to carry the redstone signal further.

Fig. 3: Jeb traps have been around a long time. Although they look complicated, with a few practice attempts, you'll be a pro and all your friends will want you to make one for them.

Fig. 4: Use sticky pistons in order for the extra blocks to retract with the piston. This method of hiding your door may be a temporary fix while you craft a more permanent solution on your server.

Fig. 5: Place an additional grass or dirt block in front of the lever to truly disguise it from unwanted company. Jot down the coordinates to make sure you remember the location of the secret door.

Construction Zone

To complete this quest, Minecrafters and their families
will engineer solutions to various challenges.

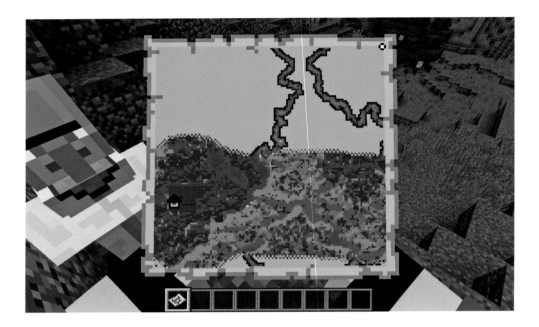

In this lab, learn how to find north with a couple of sticks, and navigate back home in Minecraft.

GO BEYOND

- Design and build a sundial clock.
- Research why the Sun rises in the east and sets in the west.
- Explore the shadow of Kukulkan at Chichen Itza, built by the Mayans, during an equinox.

WHAT'S THE SCIENCE?

The science behind this activity involves cardinal directions to track the Sun to find north. The Sun's position in the sky can be used to determine east and west. By placing the first stick in the ground, a shadow is cast. While waiting for the shadow, the Earth is rotating on its axis. The tip of the shadow at the end of an hour creates the east–west line. Once east and west are known, north and south can be found at a 90-degree angle. As the Earth rotates on its axis, the Sun rises in the east and sets in the west.

It's instinctual to want to know where we are in the world. Our devices know where we are using not only global positioning satellites (GPS) but also cell towers and Wi-Fi hotspots to approximate our location—but what happens when the battery runs out? Complete this lab and you'll always know how to find north, south, east, and west using a couple of easily gathered items.

- **APPROXIMATE TIME TO COMPLETE**
  1 hour

- **MATERIALS**
  Two 1-yard (1 m) sticks
  2 rocks

1. **Place one stick in the ground in an outdoor sunny spot. Set your first rock at the end of the shadow (fig. 1).**

2. **Wait at least 30 minutes (longer is better) and set the second rock at the end of the shadow (fig. 2).**

3. **Place the second stick in front of both rocks (fig. 3). Stand with your heels at the rocks facing away from the stick. You are facing north. Draw a line in the ground to mark north (fig. 4). This is also the basis of how a sundial clock works.**

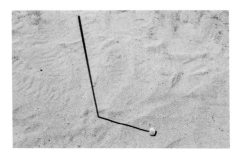

Fig. 1: The first vertical stick should cast a long shadow. Use the first rock to mark the end of the shadow. This first rock will become the westerly point.

Fig. 2: Place the second rock to mark the easterly shadow point.

Fig. 3: Place the second stick across the two rocks. We are connecting the westerly rock with the easterly rock.

Fig. 4: To make it easier to see north, draw a perpendicular line that intersects the stick lying across the front of the two rocks.

SKETCHNOTE CHALLENGE
Sketch the effect of the shadow cast by your stick.

When roaming the wilds of Minecraft, we need to remember how to get back to our home and the cool places we discover. Minecraft has cardinal directions—north, south, east and west—just as in real life. Coordinates play a key role in building our Minecraft maps. By using them, we can keep track of our finds while we explore and still make it back to our safe house before the mean mobs arrive.

■ **GAME MODE**
Creative

■ **APPROXIMATE TIME TO COMPLETE**
45 minutes

FIND IT ONLINE
Check out this video on coordinates from OMGCraft:
https://goo.gl/TL7tk1

Fig. 1: With the Sun setting in the west, you can see that sunflowers always face east. The Sun rises in the east and sets in the west.

Fig. 2: On PC Minecraft only, you can use the debug screen to find your coordinates. The colored cursor in the middle of the screen tells you which direction you're headed in.

1. **On PC/Mac/Linux version of Minecraft, press the F3 key to launch the debug screen. In the Pocket Edition, we don't have the debug screen, so we can use other features. Clouds move from east to west. The Sun rises in the east and sets in the west. Sunflowers always face east (fig. 1).**

2. **You can tell where the Sun and Moon are by crafting a clock. The hand on the clock points to the Sun or Moon, depending on whether it's day or night.**

3. **In the debug screen on PC Minecraft, which shows in text format the player's map coordinates and other information, the cursor changes to a red, green, and blue axis pointer. Red points east, green points up, and blue points south. Jot down your coordinates. After you've written down your coordinates you can walk your way back. When walking east, your *x*-coordinate increases. When moving north, your *z*-coordinate decreases (fig. 2).**

4. Craft a map and place it in your hand to reveal the surrounding terrain. Craft a zoomed-out map by placing paper around a crafted map. You can do this up to four times to craft a map that reveals over a 4-million-block radius (fig. 3).

5. Two explorer maps were added in version 1.11. To obtain an explorer map, find a cartographer villager. Cartographers wear white clothing and trade emeralds for explorer maps (fig. 4).

6. Trade with the cartographer until they give you an explorer map. You can get a woodland-explorer map that leads you to a huge woodland mansion or an ocean-monument explorer map that leads you to an underwater ocean mansion (see image on page 46). The woodland or ocean monument may be thousands of blocks away from your position. If you are off the map, you are a white dot. The map uses cardinal directions, so if the white dot is on the right-hand side of the map, you need to head west to find the monument.

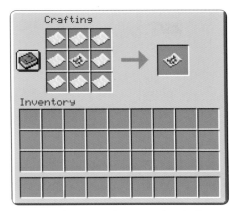

Fig. 3: Craft a zoomed-out map by placing a map in the center of your crafting table, surrounded by paper.

Fig. 4: Finding a cartographer villager isn't easy. You'll have to keep an eye out at every village you encounter. Some villagers that wear white are librarians, not cartographers.

NOW TRY THIS

Craft Elytra wings and attempt to continuously fly to populate a map with maximum zoom.

Can you name all the colors found in a rainbow? How is a rainbow created? Let's discover the answer to both these questions by creating a colorful light spectrum, in-game using beacons. Out-of-game, create a gooey slime that glows in the dark!

WHAT'S THE SCIENCE?

The goo that you created exists in a very strange state. It feels like a solid *and* a liquid. When a substance behaves this way, scientists refer to it as a *non-Newtonian fluid*.

The paint contains a substance known as phosphors. Phosphors become energized by light and then slowly release that energy by glowing for several minutes afterward.

Family Activity: Glowing Goo

Finally, a chance to get your hands gooey! In this activity, you'll make some slimy colored goo that glows in the dark. This recipe produces two sizable handfuls of goo. Pay attention to the amounts indicated or you may end up with a handful of sludge.

■ **APPROXIMATE TIME TO COMPLETE**

15 minutes + at least 1 hour to charge the glow-in-the-dark paint

■ **MATERIALS**

Mixing bowl
Spatula (optional)
1½ cups (350 ml) marshmallow creme (such as Marshmallow Fluff) or melted marshmallows
1½ cups (350 ml) cornstarch
2 ounces (50 ml) glow-in-the-dark craft acrylic paint
Bright light source

1. **In a mixing bowl, combine the marshmallow creme or melted marshmallows and 1 cup (235 ml) of the cornstarch. Use your hands or a spatula to mix until a soft dough-like goo forms (fig 1).**

2. **Add the paint to the goo, drizzling in a little at a time (fig. 2). Fold the paint into the goo until fully blended. If the goo is too sticky, add more cornstarch.**

3. **The goo needs to be placed near a bright, consistent light source for an hour or more to fully charge (fig. 3).**

Fig. 1: Combine the marshmallow and cornstarch to form a soft dough.

Fig. 2: Add the paint a little at a time, folding it in as you go. If the goo is too sticky after adding the paint, add more cornstarch.

Fig. 3: Leave the fully mixed goo under a bright light source for at least an hour to charge.

Fig. 4: Turn off the lights and enjoy your glowing goo.

 STAY SAFE!

IMPORTANT NOTES FOR PARENTS AND KIDS:

- Do *not* consume the goo! Although food ingredients are used to make it, it should *not* be eaten!
- Parents should supervise this project, especially for young children. Make sure kids don't put their hands in their mouths when handling the ingredients.
- This slime should be thrown out after 1–2 days.

4. **After sufficient time has passed to charge the goo, it's time to turn off the lights (fig. 4)!**

Minecraft beacons are used to shine a bright light high into the sky, which provides players a landmark to return to. In survival mode, they can also affect nearby players in numerous ways.

In this activity, you'll place seven beacons in a row and use colored glass to create a spectrum, which includes the colors of the rainbow. You'll want to assemble your beacon tower near the laboratory you created in Lab 1, preferably on top of a hill or mountain.

■ **GAME MODE**
Creative

■ **APPROXIMATE TIME TO COMPLETE**
1 hour

1. Beacons are found in your creative inventory. In order for them to work, you will need to place them in the center and on top of a pyramid of metal blocks: iron, gold, diamond, or emerald. The simplest pyramid is made on one level in a 3 × 3 pattern, while the most complicated one is created with a 9 × 9 base and has four levels (fig. 1).

2. Construct the bases for seven 3 × 3 pyramids adjacent to each other. You don't need any space between each pyramid base, so the foundation will be 7 × 3 blocks. Place your beacons in the center of each 3 × 3 section (fig. 2). *Tip:* If your game has cheats enabled, you can turn day into night by typing in the following command: /time set night.

3. Look carefully at the illustration of the rainbow (fig. 3). Its colors are arranged in a specific order. Starting from the left, what are they? Scientists use a memory trick to remember the order of the colors. Remember the name, Roy G. Biv, where R is red, O is orange, Y is yellow, G is green, B is blue, I is indigo, and V is violet. It turns out that Minecraft includes blocks representing each of these colors. Open your creative inventory and first find, then place, these stained-glass blocks on top of each beacon in the correct order (fig. 4):

- Red stained glass
- Orange stained glass
- Yellow stained glass
- Green stained glass
- Light blue stained glass
- Blue stained glass
  (very close to the color indigo)
- Purple stained glass

SKETCHNOTE CHALLENGE

The memory trick scientists use to remember the colors of a rainbow is called a *mnemonic* (pronounced: new-monic). There are lots of mnemonics in science; see Lab 23 (page 128) for another example. In your sketchnote journal, draw what you think Roy G. Biv might look like if he were a real person.

Is it possible to create a full spectrum using just one beacon and no redstone? What would that look like? Sketch your idea, then build it in Minecraft.

4. Time to make an even bolder statement. Remember the name? Locate the corresponding wool blocks in your inventory and cover up each pyramid (fig. 5).

5. Fly back to your laboratory and take a look. Is Roy G. Biv shining brightly in the night sky (see image on page 50) Scientist have discovered that light we see as white is actually a combination of *all* the colors of the rainbow. If you shine a bright flashlight through a prism, you'll see our old friend appear *(https://goo.gl/BAOq7o)*.

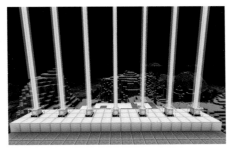

Fig. 1: Beacons must be placed on top of one of four pyramids constructed from iron, diamond, gold, or emerald blocks.

Fig. 2: Beacons must be evenly distributed. We used blocks of iron for our foundation.

NOW TRY THIS

Pistons cannot move beacons directly, but they can move other blocks. Experiment and determine a way to use pistons, redstone, and daylight sensors to activate each of your beacons when night falls. Experiment with mixing colors of stained glass. What happens if you place a light blue stained glass block on top of a yellow block?

Fig. 3: The colors of the rainbow: red, orange, yellow, green, blue, indigo, violet.

Fig. 4: Hold down the shift key and right-click to place a stained-glass block on top of a beacon.

Fig. 5: Cover each pyramid with colored wool to match the beacon color.

FIND IT ONLINE

Here's a link to an impressive beacon tower created by YouTuber CR3W, who figured out how to use redstone mechanisms and circuitry to simulate a beautiful rainbow beacon: *https://goo.gl/HeaeDz*

This lab is all about crystals: how they form, the shapes they take, and how they fit together. In the hands-on activity, you'll create colorful crystals out of laundry detergent. In the Minecraft challenge, you'll build a giant crystal castle using ice, quartz, diamonds, and emeralds.

FIND IT ONLINE

- We love this video that demonstrates how ice crystals are formed in mineral water: *https://goo.gl/UbzCuc*

WHAT'S THE SCIENCE?

Epsom salt contains the chemical magnesium sulfate and forms a crystal structure. When it is mixed with warm water, the structure breaks down. As the solution cools, the atoms reform into another crystal structure.

Family Activity: Make Your Own Crystals

In this lab, you'll witness how crystals grow and take the shape of a beautifully colored snowflake.

■ **APPROXIMATE TIME TO COMPLETE**

1 hour, plus time for crystals to form

■ **MATERIALS**

Epsom salt, in a 1:1 ratio with water
(we used 8 ounces/236.6 ml water
to 1 cup/250 ml salt crystals)

2 or 3 wide-mouth, deep jars or
drinking glasses

Food coloring (optional)

Warm water

Stirring sticks

Scissors (optional)

Several white ¼-inch (6 mm)
pipe cleaners

Several blue ¼-inch (6 mm)
pipe cleaners (optional)

String or fishing line

Pencils

Fig. 1: Pipe cleaners suspended in a solution of Epsom salt crystals and warm water will create beautiful snowflakes.

Fig. 2: Suspend the pipe cleaners in a super-saturated solution of Epsom salt and water. Food coloring is optional.

Fig. 3: Form snowflake shapes with pipe cleaners. You can create one snowflake per jar.

Fig. 4: Colorful crystals will begin to form on the pipe cleaners after several hours. Remove from the solution when you are satisfied with the crystal development.

1. Gather your materials (fig. 1). Pour Epsom salt solution into each jar. Add food coloring, if desired. Pour warm tap water into each jar and stir rapidly until the crystals are completely dissolved. You want to create a super-saturated solution, which means crystals remain at the bottom even after vigorous stirring (fig. 2).

2. Cut or twist the pipe cleaners down to size, as needed to fit into your jars. Twist them into the shape of random snowflakes, and suspend them in each jar using string and a pencil (fig. 3).

3. Place the jars in a safe location, or in the refrigerator, where they will not be disturbed. Within 24 hours, you should have a healthy colony of crystals developing on your snowflakes (fig. 4). Remove from the solution when you are satisfied and hang in a bright place to catch the light.

You may want to call in lots of family and friends for this activity. The challenge is to build a sizable castle in a cold biome out of giant crystals of various shapes. You should use mostly ice, both packed ice and regular ice, but diamonds, emeralds, and quartz are crystals, too, so use a few of those, as well. We'll show you what each type of crystal would look like if built in Minecraft, then it's your challenge to create a castle using as many of the crystal shapes as you can.

- **GAME MODE**
  Creative

- **APPROXIMATE TIME TO COMPLETE**
  2–3 hours

SKETCHNOTE CHALLENGE

Venture outside when you get a chance and go on a crystal hunt. Perhaps there is a local rock club that can share samples with you, or visit a local gem and mineral shop or attend an event at a rock and gem show. Sketch several of each type and label them as you go.

1. **Pick a location in a cold biome. Bonus if there are already ice spikes growing (fig. 1).**

2. **Cubic crystal: This is the easiest and provides the most options. Make your cubic crystals with 6, 8, or 12 sides. They can be made of ice or diamonds (fig. 2).**

3. **Hexagonal crystal: These have a familiar shape for Minecraft players. They can be made of ice, emerald, or quartz blocks (fig. 3).**

Fig. 1: Look for a site that already has ice spikes to build your castle.

Fig. 2: The cubic shape is easiest. Build several sizes and use different types of blocks.

Fig. 3: The hexagon shape would make excellent tall towers.

Fig. 4: The monoclinic shape looks strange in Minecraft, like a staircase to nowhere.

Fig. 5: Build a pyramid and attach another one to the bottom.

4. Monoclinic crystal: These look like a box that is about to fall over. These should be made of ice (fig. 4).

5. Orthorhombic crystal: Attach two Minecraft pyramids together at their bases (fig. 5).

6. Tetragonal crystal: Stretch out a cube and attach a pyramid on either end. These should be made of ice (fig. 6).

7. Triclinic crystal: Just about anything goes with these. They tend to be flatter than the others and have multiple sides (fig. 7).

8. Build your castle out of an assortment of crystal shapes. Some can be standing up, others lying down. Set a few on their edges and some should lie flat. Add lighting, but be careful with torches and lava near ice. Packed ice won't melt, but regular ice will and make quite a mess. Put in stairs, ladders, doors, and windows to suit your taste.

9. Refer to the image on page 54 to see how we built our castle out of giant crystals.

Fig. 6: These tetragonal crystals can be extra large in size. Begin with an upside-down pyramid for the base.

Fig. 7: Triclinic crystals have a very peculiar shape with many sides. Use these to fill in any gaps.

NOW TRY THIS

- We added a bit of lava to our castle. Modify this build to make it a fire and ice castle.
- Turn this build into a fun parkour map. Sliding on ice can make it much more difficult.

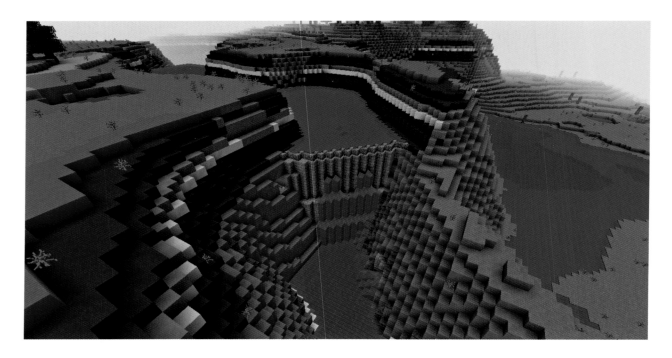

Waves aren't limited to water crashing at the beach. Actually, waves are all around us. For instance, the colors we see with our eyes have traveled in visible color waves, and the signal on your cellphone travels in radio waves.

In this lab, you'll study waves in a homemade wave pool and build a water dam inside Minecraft. There are a few key terms to understand before we dive into waves: crest, trough, wavelength, amplitude, and frequency (see "What's the Science?" on page 59).

Special tools are required to study the invisible radio waves that surround us every day. On the other hand, using a few household materials will enable you to create and study water waves.

■ **APPROXIMATE TIME TO COMPLETE**
45 minutes

■ **MATERIALS**
Baking pan
Sand
Water
Ruler

Fig. 1: A disposable aluminum casserole dish works great as a wave pool. Use a pan that's at least 3 inches (7.6 cm) deep.

Fig. 2: Add water to the pan slowly to prevent beach erosion. You'll change the shape of the beach later

1. Use a deep-walled baking pan to help prevent water from spilling over the sides. Place the baking pan on a level surface. (fig. 2)

2. Spread sufficient sand on one side of the pan to create a small artificial beach. Pour water to create a pool approximately 2 inches (5 cm) deep (fig. 2). Reshape the sand beach to one side of the pan, if needed. Let the water settle and measure the water depth.

3. One person should hold the ruler along the side of the pan while the other creates waves. Use the palm of your hand to push into the water. Measure the crest and valley of the waves. Try different types of hand positions as well as stronger or lighter force (fig. 3).

4. Create a different base for the waves by adding sand to the other side of the pan. Shape the sand under the water to explore new waveforms (fig. 4)

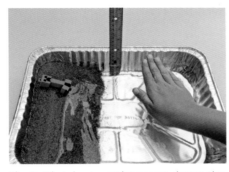

Fig. 3: What do you notice as you change the shape of your hand? Using a camera to record the waves makes it easier to see the crest and valley of the waves.

Fig. 4: Add more sand to the other side of the pan. Shape the sand under the water to create various waveforms.

WHAT'S THE SCIENCE?

The high point of a wave is the *crest*, or peak, while its low point is the *trough*. Whenever there's a disturbance (such as wind), the response is typically a wave traveling outward. As the waves get closer to shore, they create breaking waves, which are affected by the shape of the beach. *Wavelength* is the distance between the high points of a wave. *Amplitude* is the height of the peak or the depth of the trough from the baseline. *Frequency* is the amount of peaks and troughs in a given area in a second. To learn more about visible spectrum waves, check out Lab 6 (see page 50).

Although there are no waves in Minecraft, we can use our imagination with the unique characteristics of water, in-game, while building a dam. Dams are built to retain only a certain amount of water and to release excess water through spillways or floodgates. When it rains and the water level behind the dam rises, the floodgates open to release water. Ungated dams have spillways that allow water to spill over a specific height of the dam.

■ **GAME MODE**
Creative

■ **APPROXIMATE TIME TO COMPLETE**
45 minutes

FIND IT ONLINE
- Use this link to find specific biomes: *http://chunkbase.com/apps/biome-finder*
- Check out HermitCraft's dam, which operates based on sunlight: *https://goo.gl/PGM31K*

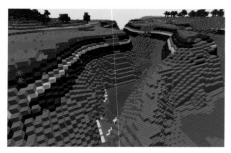

Fig. 1: Mesa biomes make great areas to create a dam. The dry landscape is a stark contrast to the water flowing in the river and behind the dam.

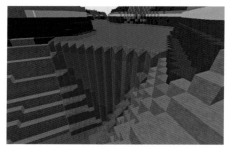

Fig. 2: The floating dirt layer is a quick way to make the water behind your dam appear very deep. Find a level that makes the dam seem very full and build a dirt block layer.

1. Explore a creative world to find a worthy canyon in a Mesa biome (fig. 1). See Find It Online, below, for a link to find specific biomes. If you can't find a Mesa biome, try an amplified biome or a plains biome.

2. Use the unique features of water to your advantage. Start by filling the canyon with water. A trick is to build a layer of dirt the level you want the water. Pour lots of water buckets on top of the dirt (fig. 2).

3. Where the water cascade ends, start building the dam. Dams typically angle back toward the water. The lowest level is stepped away from the water, while the second and third levels are tiered back toward the water.

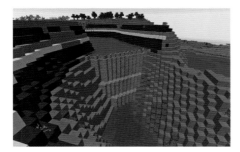

Fig. 3: For visual effect, craft the dam with stone bricks, cracked stone bricks, and mossy stone bricks. Switch between the three types of blocks for a naturally weathered-looking dam.

Fig. 4: The redstone build area is below the water level behind the dam. Look carefully to see water dripping from the ceiling.

Fig. 5: Between the mossy blocks you can see the sticky pistons. The two sticky pistons move mossy stone bricks to close the dam. The piston on the left has a mossy stone brick, while the one on the right is waiting for one.

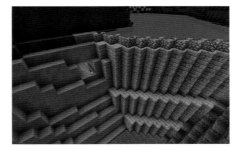

Fig. 6: The finished dam.

4. Finish the third layer of the dam 1 block below the water level. Top the dam with cobblestone wall and mossy cobblestone wall. You should have a dam built to the water level with 3 tiered levels (fig. 3).

5. To build the redstone dam gates, create a corridor behind the dam. Redstone breaks when it gets wet, so be sure to craft a dry area for all your redstone items (fig. 4).

6. Break an area large enough in the front of the dam to add sticky piston gates. Add sticky pistons and build a small water source to release the water when the pistons are deactivated. Place a stone block on the end of the sticky pistons to blend in with the dam (fig. 5).

7. Place a lever in a convenient location to activate/deactivate the sticky pistons. Tunnel to the side of the dam, and place redstone dust and repeaters to reach the lever. Flip the lever to release the flood down the dam and into the river (fig. 6).

NOW TRY THIS

- Craft a working dam that automatically waters crops.
- Build a Kundt's tube, a device used by scientists, to demonstrate standing waves: *https://goo.gl/cMJqKw*
- Research and build an oscilloscope in Minecraft using repeaters.

QUEST 3

The Sky Is Not Your Limit

To complete this quest, Minecrafters and their families will look to the sky for inspiration.

Mars Space Station

In this lab, you'll consider which materials you'll take to Mars—the fourth planet from the Sun—to build habitats for humans, both in and out of the game.

For the family activity, you'll work with your playing partner(s) to design a model Mars habitat for humans.

WHAT'S THE SCIENCE?

Your habitats must address Mars's severe conditions:

- Its atmosphere contains less than 1% oxygen.
- Its atmospheric pressure is less than 1% of Earth's, so it can't support liquid water.
- Its gravity is 37.5% of Earth's.
- It has no magnetic field, so the surface has no protection from the Sun's radiation.
- Average temperatures at its equator range from −100°F to 67°F (−73°C to 20°C).
- It has frequent wind and dust storms.

Your Mars habitats must include everything humans, animals, and crops will need to survive.

- How will you design and build these habitats?
- How will lower gravity affect your build?
- Mars is about 225 million km—nearly 140 million miles—from Earth, so it can take a resupply mission more than 6 months to reach your colony. What supplies will you take with you on your first voyage? How will you plan to recycle and reuse those supplies?

Family Activity: Model Mars Habitat

■ **APPROXIMATE TIME TO COMPLETE**

45 minutes

■ **MATERIALS**

Craft acrylic paints in various colors

Paintbrush(es)

Toilet paper tubes

Styrofoam shapes (we used cones and half balls)

Aluminum foil

Bamboo skewers or toothpicks

Transparent tape

Empty plastic containers (optional)

Gummy candy (optional)

Pipe cleaners (optional)

Plastic wrap (optional)

Large sheet of cardboard (for mounting your habitat)

Mylar wrapping paper or sheets (or the inside of an old Mylar balloon)

1. Read "What's the Science" to learn about Mars's environment. As you gather your materials, think about how you might use them to create a habitat that can withstand those conditions and protect humans.

2. Design and build basic structures. Include places to sleep, eat, grow food, and conduct research and experiments (fig. 1). All human activity on Mars must be done indoors.

Fig. 1: Design and build structures for sleeping, eating, and farming.

Fig. 2: Devise new layouts to improve your design or to address other needs or uses.

3. *Iterate,* or repeat, your model by adding to and/or changing the layout to better suit your mission or to address needs or uses you and your partner(s) hadn't thought of when you started (fig. 2). We changed our layout so our living habitat would be closer to our farm habitat and used our first model for other purposes. When scientists start an experiment, they begin with a *hypothesis*, or assumption, based on their observations, but they don't expect a specific outcome. Scientists always test their ideas, then retest to explore different results that could also prove useful. This process is known as *iteration* (see page 66).

Fig. 3: Mount your finished models on a cardboard base.

4. Mount your finished models on a sheet of cardboard. We covered our cardboard with red Mylar so it would look like Mars's red surface (fig. 3).

Your rocket ship has landed in a Mars-like Mesa biome. The clay blocks of a Mesa biome look similar to the red dust that covers Mars's surface. All around you are materials you can use to build your colony.

■ **GAME MODE**
Survival

■ **APPROXIMATE TIME TO COMPLETE**
1-2 hours

■ **PLATFORMS**
PC/Mac, Consoles, PE

 FIND IT ONLINE
• We expect humans to land on and colonize Mars in our lifetimes. NASA (the National Aeronautics and Space Administration) has challenged scientists to design housing for space travel using 3D printing, to create recycling systems, and to build complete habitats. Learn more here: *https://goo.gl/FY2V4s*
• To learn more about and play games inspired by Mars, check out NASA's Mars Exploration Funzone: *https://goo.gl/zWHpJf*

1. **You've landed on Mars with your rocketship full of materials. Your crew on Earth packed your rocket with the following material (fig. 1):**
   • *Gold—8x Gold Ingot.* Gold is one of the best conductors of electricity. Most of your electronics will have some gold in them. Melt down no-longer-used electronics to repurpose the gold for your build.
   • *Iron.* Modern rockets use various alloyed metals. An alloyed metal is a blend of different metals that makes it strong. Since Minecraft doesn't offer alloy metals, we'll use iron. Actually, Mars gets its red color from the iron oxide found in the soil, so you'll be able to use extra iron extracted from Mars's soil.
   • *Glass—15x glass blocks.*
   • *Fuel—64x coal.*
   • *Tools—1x iron shovel, 1x compass, 1x flint and steel, 1x iron pickaxe.*
   • *Food—25x potatoes, 64x wheat seeds, 32x apples, 15x cookies, 1x cake, 64x bread, 64x beetroot seeds.*
   • *Water—5 buckets of water.*
   • *Crockery—5x bowls, 1x empty bucket.*
   • *Parts—64x wood sticks, 1x furnace.*
   • *Miscellaneous—1x rocket-propelled Elytra, 1x bed, 64x redstone dust, and 10 blocks of your choice.*

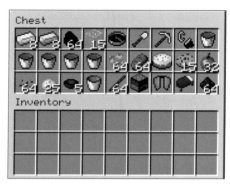

Fig. 1: The rocketship inventory for your Mars build.

GO BEYOND
Players seeking more of a challenge can try these calculations:
• If you weigh 80 pounds (36.3 kg) on Earth, you would weigh only 30 pounds (13.6 kg) on Mars. Think of how high you could jump, and how little it would hurt if you fell while riding a bike! To find your exact weight on Mars, multiply your Earth weight by 0.375.
• Measure the volume of your habitats. A comfortable living space is at least 71.7 square yards (60 square m) per person.

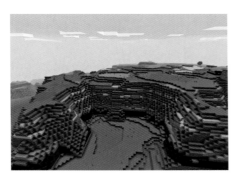

Fig. 2: An overview of the Mars/Mesa biome.

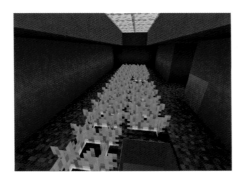

Fig. 3: An indoor Mars garden.

Fig. 4: An underground living space.

2. The soil on Mars is covered in materials you can use as part of your build. On Mars, you would find sand, granite, slate, carbon dioxide, and iron dust. Your in-game Mars Mesa biome is made up of red sand, hardened clay, and stained clay (fig. 2).

3. Explore the Mesa biome to find the best spot to start building your Mars habitats. You'll need enough land area to build multiple habitats. The sizes of your various habitats will depend on how many people are on your mission and how you use the materials. Start by building a habitat for growing food. Since Mars has almost no atmosphere, food cannot grow outside. Design and build an area to grow enough food to survive (fig. 3).

4. Next, build a habitat for living. Your living quarters need to include a place to eat, sleep, and relax. Get creative with the design of your living quarters. Build it underground for ultimate protection from the harsh Mars environment (fig. 4).

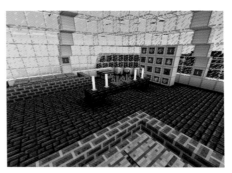

Fig. 5: A research facility for studying your findings on Mars.

5. Every Mars expedition will have a research facility to study the soil, rocks, and other materials you discover and gather (fig. 5). Part of your mission is to learn about the history of Mars. It's believed that Mars once had water. Where did that water go? Is it all frozen underground?

6. Iterate your build to prepare for future Mars astronauts. As the first humans to colonize Mars, you expect other people will follow your example. Consider building larger habitats, stocking food, and exploring and building habitats far from your home base.

Elytra are beetles' hardened forewings and were added to the PC version of Minecraft 1.9. Elytra allow players to glide and are incredibly fun in amplified biomes. It may be faster for a beetle to open its wings and fly, but it will still encounter air resistance.

In this lab, you'll design gliding wings for your Minecraft character to be tested on a homemade zipline. You'll experience air resistance, a type of friction that will affect your Elytra zipline creation.

To stay true to the Elytra theme, we're going to create a beetle with various Elytra shapes. We'll test large Elytra, small Elytra, and irregular-shaped Elytra. You'll need an open area to set up your Elytra zipline. If your object stops before it reaches the end, it has experienced too much friction.

Consider papercrafting your Minecraft character. To learn how to make a foldable 3D paper character, check out Lab 13 (page 82), Creating Figures, in *Unofficial Minecraft Lab for Kids*.

 FIND IT ONLINE

To see friction at work, check out Colin Furze's bike with ice wheels: *https://goo.gl/n9QE41*

■ **APPROXIMATE TIME TO COMPLETE**
30 minutes

■ **MATERIALS**
Cardboard
Crayons or markers
Masking tape
Weights, such as coins
String
Paper clip

1. Gather your supplies (fig. 1). On the cardboard, design and color three types of Elytra wings: small, large, and irregular (fig 2). Use tape to attach the wings to a weighted object.

2. Stretch your string from a high to a low point. Open up a paper clip and attach one end to the wings (fig. 3).

3. Hang the other end on the paper clip on the string (fig. 4). Adjust the tightness and angle of the string to make your Elytra fly down the string.

4. What can you change on the wings to make them move faster along your zipline? What can you do to the string to make your wings move faster? Consider changing the shape of the Elytra, the weight on the Elytra, the way the Elytra hangs, and the surface the Elytra hangs on to make it move faster along the zipline.

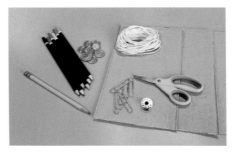

Fig. 1: Gather materials to build a zipline and Elytra-type flying objects. Substitute any materials for items you have on hand.

Fig. 2: Design different types of Elytra.

Fig. 3: Bend and attach paper clips to create a hanger for the Elytra to glide down the zipline.

Fig. 4: Test your Elytra on the zipline.

WHAT'S THE SCIENCE?
Friction, air resistance, drag, and lift are important concepts to understand in this lab. Without *friction* your feet would slip with every step. Low friction is like walking on ice. Friction is what slows a bicycle when coasting. Friction creates fire when two sticks are rubbed together. *Air resistance*, also called *drag*, can be thought of as friction. As the air flows over and under the wings, friction is created between the wing and the air. This airflow also creates *lift*, the force that allows things to fly.

Let's experiment with the principles of flight when using Elytra in Minecraft. For this lab, we'll go up 10-block intervals and attempt to fly out as far as possible. Create a chart to record your flight distances.

It takes practice to engage your Elytra wings immediately after leaping off your tower. Adjust your angle of attack for greater flight distances.

■ **GAME MODE**
Creative or survival

■ **APPROXIMATE TIME TO COMPLETE**
30 minutes

GO BEYOND

Learn more about the principles of flight, including lift, drag, thrust, and weight.

COLUMN HEIGHT (IN M)	PREFLIGHT DISTANCE ESTIMATE (IN M)	ELYTRA SOARING DISTANCE (IN M)
10	50	23
20	150	110
30	225	212
40	250	305
50	325	405

1. Equip your character with Elytra in the chestplate slot. If playing in survival mode, Elytra can be found in end cities. If playing in creative mode, Elytra are found in the transportation tab that looks like redstone-powered rail (fig. 1).

2. Build a tower 50 blocks high with jumping stations every 10 blocks. We used white and black wool to help count the height of the blocks (fig. 2).

3. Set up measuring blocks along the flight path. Use colorful blocks to help mark numbered intervals. Use black wool every 10 blocks and another color to mark the added distance (fig. 3).

4. Before you fly off your tower, write down your estimates about how far in blocks (meters) you will fly. Get curious about how far you might be able to fly from each jumping point.

5. Have your chart handy as you leap and fly from each Elytra platform. Jot down your distance, relative to your starting platform height. To enable Elytra jump, in midair (fig. 4).

6. As a scientist, you should test your results multiple times, not just to get as a far as possible but also to learn about Elytra flight.

7. Graph and color your data on a chart. Make your *y*-axis your column jumping height and your *x*-axis the distance in blocks you traveled.

Fig. 1: Once Elytra are equipped and you are flying, go into your inventory for funny images of your character.

Fig. 2: Build jumping stations every 10 blocks. Add a ladder to the back for easy climbing.

Fig. 3: We love the feeling of flying with Elytra. See how far you can fly along the measuring field.

Fig. 4: Enable third-person view by pressing the F5 key while gliding down the measurement for even more fun. Craft and use rockets to fly forever!

NOW TRY THIS

- What can you add to your object to make it fly up the zipline?
- What can you take away from your object to make it fly faster along the zipline?
- To make your Elytra fly, not just glide, craft and use a firework while in Elytra flight. To learn more about rockets, check out Lab 12 (page 76).

ELYTRA SOARING DISTANCE VS. COLUMN HEIGHT

■ Elytra Soaring Distance in Meters

Column Height (vertical axis): 10, 20, 30, 40, 50

Elytra Soaring Distance in Meters (horizontal axis): 0, 100, 200, 300, 400, 500

Weather is the condition of the atmosphere, which is the layer of gas that surrounds the Earth. Our weather is influenced by many factors, including wind, temperature, and humidity. Climate is the overall pattern for each area and it determines which plants can grow.

The atmosphere is made up of five main layers. From Earth looking toward space, the atmosphere is separated into the troposphere, stratosphere, mesosphere, thermosphere, exosphere, and then space. We live in the troposphere and breathe a mixture of 78 percent nitrogen, 21 percent oxygen, 1 percent water vapor, and other trace elements. Step outside and look up. See any clouds? That's condensed water vapor. In this lab, we'll study the effects of condensation of water vapor, that 1 percent of our atmosphere.

WHAT'S THE SCIENCE?

Clouds are made up of tiny drops of water. They're formed as the Sun heats up the ground and the warm air begins to rise. As the warm air rises, the water vapor cools and condenses into water droplets. We can visually experiment with condensation using a glass and ice water. As the water drops grow larger, they become heavier and slide down the glass or fall from the cloud. Next time it rains, think about how condensed water vapor became the drops falling on your head. Get curious about weather. Why doesn't it rain in a desert? What creates dramatic weather like storms, hurricanes, and tornadoes?

With a few materials, we'll see the effects of condensation to understand how clouds are formed and why rain falls. Is it cloudy outside today? What type of clouds do you see?

- ◼ **APPROXIMATE TIME TO COMPLETE**

  1 hour

- ◼ **MATERIALS**

  A glass

  Bowl

  Ice

  Water

  Watch or timer

  Silicone spatula (optional)

  Measuring cup

1. **Water vapor appears to be a mystery because it's tough to see until it condenses. Let's make the invisible, visible, with some simple items you likely have at home (fig. 1).**

2. **Place the glass in a bowl. Add ice, then water to fill the glass. Check the time and note how long it takes for water vapor to condense into droplets on the side of the glass (fig. 2). Our room temperature was 80°F (26.7°C) with 65 percent humidity. Record the time, room temperature, and humidity in your science sketchbook to keep track of your observations. You can use a weather app or website to tell the temperature and humidity.**

Fig. 1: Although any cup will work, a clear glass works great to easily see the amount of condensation that collects.

3. **Note how long it takes until the water droplets start to run down the side of the glass (fig. 3).**

4. **Measure how much water condensed on the outside of your glass in this time frame. This step can be difficult, so take care to collect as much of the condensed water as possible. Using your finger or a silicone spatula, wipe the condensation on the glass into the collection bowl (fig. 4). Next, pour the accumulated water from your collection bowl into a measuring cup.**

 FIND IT ONLINE

For a quick cloud matching game, visit *https://goo.gl/noXRhj*

Fig. 2: It took about 10 minutes for the first drops of condensation to gather on the side of the glass.

Fig. 3: After about 30 minutes, water condensation has started to run down the glass.

Fig. 4: After 1 hour, with plenty of water streaks, we're ready to measure how much water has condensed on the glass. We collected a little less than 1 teaspoon (4 ml) off the glass.

In Minecraft, clouds always hover at around 130 meters (142 yards), yet rain and snow originate much higher than the clouds. The temperature biomes determine whether it will rain, snow, or remain dry. Just like real life, low temperatures create snow, mid-temperatures create rain, and high temperatures, like those found in a desert biome, will have no precipitation.

You've likely experienced rain and a thunderstorm, in-game, but what other elements have you noticed that contribute to the weather in Minecraft?

■ **GAME MODE**
Creative

■ **APPROXIMATE TIME TO COMPLETE**
45 minutes

NOW TRY THIS
- If your hometown were a biome in Minecraft, which biome would it be?
- Keep your eyes open for a charged creeper (a creeper that's been struck by lightning).

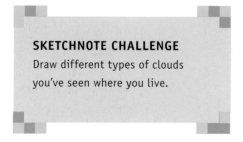

SKETCHNOTE CHALLENGE
Draw different types of clouds you've seen where you live.

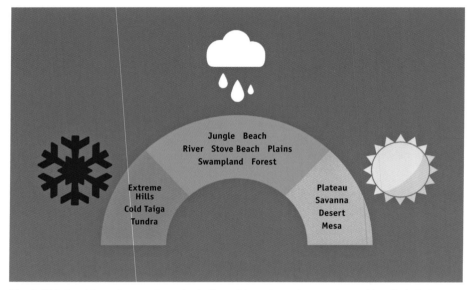

Fig. 1: This is a biome temperature chart. Every biome has a temperature rating that, in turn, causes certain types of weather.

1. Find your favorite biome, maybe the Taiga, Forest, Jungle, or Plains. As you make your way toward your favorite biome, observe the weather patterns in the biomes you pass through. Notice in our biome graphic that biomes have temperature ratings (fig. 1).

2. What type of weather can you expect in your favorite biome (fig. 2)? Does it rain? What happens when the rain falls? What happens when you scale to a high point while it's raining? What can you make with snow in Minecraft?

3. Do you love to craft snowballs? Which biomes and altitudes have snow? What makes snow accumulate on the ground? What causes snow to melt in Minecraft (fig. 3)?

4. Lightning has several strange effects (fig. 4). Not only will it cause any flammable material to catch fire, but it also bends light. Any mob is visually hidden behind the lightning bolt. Take care near lightning because it may cause you harm and can hide hostile mobs that can cause even more harm.

5. Unlike real life, we can control weather in Minecraft. Controlling the weather is useful when we're trying to build, put out fires, or see what we're doing. To use the commands, you must be OP and have cheats enabled. The pattern for the command is /weather (clear, rain, thunder) (time in seconds). Try a few of these commands in the chat bar: /weather clear 100, /weather rain 100, /weather thunder 100. What happens when you try to make it rain in a cold biome? Can we really control the weather?

6. Meteorologists love rare weather. Rare weather in-game can be found in biomes like the Ice Plains Spikes, a cold biome where the cold is seen in the form of ice spikes. Similar to stalagmites found in caves, ice spikes are ice blocks that rise up from the ground (fig. 5). Search and record rare weather effects found in your worlds.

Fig. 2: Rain falls in warm biomes. Although the rain doesn't fill up rivers, the effect in-game looks pleasing while playing.

Fig. 3: Snow falls at high altitudes and in cold biomes. When snow falls, it doesn't always accumulate on the ground.

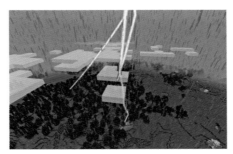

Fig. 4: Thunder and lightning are hazardous to your character's health. Take care not to get too close, but if you do, keep a close eye on the lightning because you'll find some strange game glitches.

Fig. 5: Ice Plains Spikes biomes are very rare and offer unique weather effects in-game. Once you find an Ice Plains Spikes biome, try changing the weather to rain.

GO BEYOND
- Where else does water vapor condense? How can you test the effects of water vapor on items other than a glass filled with ice water? What happens to your glass of ice water when placed in the freezer or in the snow? Why?
- Build a weather station that uploads data to a site like Weather Underground.

In this lab, you'll experiment with milk, food coloring, and dish detergent, and learn the science behind the beautiful bursts of color you can create. Then, you'll discover how to create four different kinds of fireworks in Minecraft and use dispensers, repeaters, and a comparator to set up an automated show worthy of a special celebration.

This simple experiment yields beautiful results.

- **APPROXIMATE TIME TO COMPLETE**
  30 minutes

- **MATERIALS**
  Shallow pan or baking dish
  Whole milk
  Dish detergent
  Small container or bowl for dish soap
  Food coloring in several colors
  Cotton swabs

1. **Gather your materials. Pour a thin layer of milk into the bottom of a shallow pan. Pour a small amount of dish detergent into a small container. Gently place several small drops of food coloring onto the milk (fig. 1).**

2. **Dip a cotton swab into the dish detergent, and then touch the soaked tip to a drop of food coloring (fig. 2). The detergent will immediately react with the milk, spreading the food coloring in all directions.**

3. **Repeat for each drop of food coloring. Your fireworks show will continue for several minutes (fig. 3).**

Fig. 1: Place single drops of food coloring onto the milk.

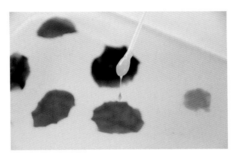
Fig. 2: Each drop of color should get one drop of dish detergent. The reaction will be immediate.

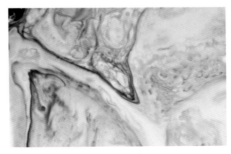
Fig. 3: As you add a drop of detergent to each drop of food coloring, the colors will explode in different directions.

WHAT'S THE SCIENCE?

Opposites attract! Because the negatively charged detergent molecules are attracted to the positively charged fat molecules in the milk, they zoom around as they connect, twisting and turning the food coloring on the milk's surface as they go.

NOW TRY THIS

You can try testing a few different *variables*. Variables are things that can be changed in an experiment.

- Compare whole milk with cream, which has a higher fat content, or with a lower-fat milk. Does the fat content affect the colorful display?
- What happens if you place the drops of color close together? Farther apart?
- What happens if you introduce a gentle disturbance?

TYPES OF FIREWORK STARS	RECIPE
Small ball	Gunpowder + Dye
Large ball	Gunpowder + Fire charge + Dye
Star shaped	Gunpowder + Gold nugget + Dye
Burst	Gunpowder + Feather + Dye

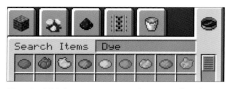

Fig. 1: Add dyes to gunpowder to make the fireworks colorful.

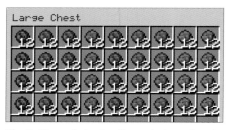

Fig. 2: We made twelve firework stars of each type and color for a really big show!

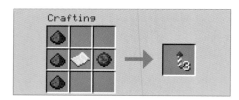

Fig. 3: The more gunpowder you use, the higher the rocket will fly and the longer it will take for the firework to explode.

Show off your master Minecrafting skills by making four different kinds of firework shells, called *firework stars,* and then attaching each to one or more rockets before firing them off with a bank of dispensers.

■ **GAME MODE**
Creative

■ **APPROXIMATE TIME TO COMPLETE**
2 hours

■ **PLATFORMS**
All

SKETCHNOTE CHALLENGE
Which of the four kinds of fireworks did you use on your rockets? Sketch the patterns that each makes and the recipe you used to create each.

1. **The four types of firework stars available are listed above, along with the crafting recipe for each. The gunpowder's grays don't make for very colorful fireworks, but you can add color by adding dyes. Search for dyes to find the colors you want to use. You can also craft blue fireworks by placing lapis lazuli into your crafting table, and red fireworks with red dye from a red rose bush. Place the items in a row in your crafting table. Substitute the color of your choice with dye (fig. 1).**

2. **Craft as many of each type of firework star as you need for your show. Start small to get the hang of it and to test out each type before you create all the fireworks for your celebration show (fig. 2).**

3. **Make your rockets by crafting one, two, or three gunpowder with paper and one of your firework stars (fig. 3). The more gunpowder, the higher the rockets will fly and the longer the firework will take to explode. You can fill the table with more firework stars and create rockets that burst in multiple colors.**

Fig. 4: Use redstone to connect each dispenser to one lever or button. If you don't want to launch all rockets at once, attach repeaters to some of the dispensers.

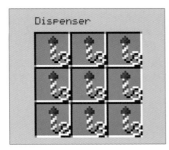

Fig. 5: Each dispenser can hold up to 64 × 9 rockets!

4. Place seven dispensers next to each other and point them at the sky. Connect each with redstone and run the redstone to a lever several blocks away. Attach repeaters to some of the dispensers to slow down the reaction time (fig. 4).

Fig. 6: Place a comparator next to the lever and create a loop of redstone, connect the redstone to the circuit, then activate the comparator by right-clicking it.

5. Pull the lever to test your circuit. If it lights up, you're ready to fire. Load each dispenser with rockets (fig. 5).

6. Launch your rockets seven at a time by pulling the lever. Reset the lever each time before launching another round. You can also launch all the dispensers in rapid-fire mode by attaching a redstone comparator to your lever. Make sure the comparator is active (right-click it), then create a loop with redstone and connect it to your circuit (fig. 6).

GO BEYOND

Players seeking more of a challenge can try:

- Experimenting with the amount of gunpowder and repeater ticks and time your show to music.
- Using a rocket to speed up flight by Elytra.
- Launching a rocket by simply using it (right-click) on top of a block.

FIND IT ONLINE

- There are several special shapes and effects that can be created with firework rockets. You can also make one color fade into another. Find the details at Minecraft Gamepedia: *https://goo.gl/SzMvLV*
- If you have a Minecraft Realm of your own, or you can join a friend's Realm, check out the amazing firework shows some very creative people have made: *https://goo.gl/2Sjb96*

Rocks, Minerals, and Gems

To complete this quest, Minecrafters and their families plant their feet firmly on the ground and dig beneath it.

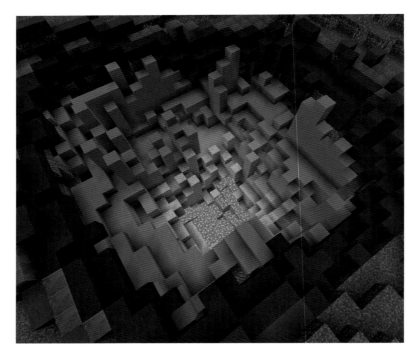

What do we have in store for you in this lab? How about a sizable encounter with geology and a delectable baking challenge that the entire family, and maybe even the neighborhood, will enjoy.

I hope you are hungry, because you and your family are going to bake a cake. And not just any cake, mind you, but a five-layer cake constructed to resemble what geologists refer to as the Earth's soil horizons. Alternately, this cake could be made with three layers, replacing layers two and four with extra frosting.

■ **APPROXIMATE TIME TO COMPLETE**
3–4 hours

■ **MATERIALS**
5 round cake pans
Nonstick cooking spray (optional)
Parchment paper
5 different cake mixes
    (see cake layers table)
1¹/₂ cups (225 g) walnuts, pecans,
    or other nuts
1¹/₂ cups (150 g) cookie crumbles
Sharp knife
Silicone spatula
Frosting of your choice, enough to
    spread between each layer and
    over the cake

WHAT'S THE SCIENCE?

Soil scientists are specialists that examine the "soil crust" of the Earth. Just beneath us are many feet of soil types. They fit into several categories based on what color they are and what they contain. They are commonly referred to as *horizons*: zones where one type is replaced by another type. Minecraft players explore soil horizons as we dig deeper in our worlds. In Minecraft, just as in real life, the final soil horizon is bedrock.

Family Activity: Soil Horizons Cake

1. Gather your ingredients (fig. 1). Spray the pans with nonstick cooking spray or line with parchment paper to avoid sticking. Bake each cake according to the directions on the package. Fold the nuts into the yellow cake and the cookie crumbs into the white cake before baking. (Most likely, each mix will make two cakes. Freeze the second cake for later use.)

2. After each cake has cooled completely, use a sharp knife to slice the crown off each to make the surface flatter (fig. 2). *Tip:* Pop each cake in the freezer for a few minutes before slicing to prevent crumbling.

3. With a silicone spatula, spread frosting on top of each layer. Stack them according to the order in the Soil Horizon cake layers table (fig. 3).

4. Frost the outside of the cake and chill for 2 hours to allow it to firm. When ready to eat, slice and enjoy your horizon cake (fig. 4)!

CAKE LAYER	CAKE TYPE	SOIL HORIZON NAME
Top layer	Chocolate	Organic, or humus layer of plant remains
Second layer	Carrot cake	Topsoil, organic matter, and minerals
Third layer	Spice cake	Subsoil, mostly clay and iron
Fourth layer	Yellow cake with nuts	Parent material, rocky layer
Bottom layer	White cake with cookie crumbles	Bedrock, massive and solid rock

Fig. 1: You'll be making 5 different cakes. Add nuts to the yellow cake and cookie crumbles to the white cake.

Fig. 2: Level each cake, as needed.

Fig. 3: Stack and frost in order according to the cake layers table.

Fig. 4: Horizon cake layers from top to bottom: organic, topsoil, subsoil, parent material, and bedrock.

In the family activity for this lab, you baked a cake that resembled the Earth's soil layers. Now it is time to cut open the Earth itself. The Earth contains four layers. At the center is the inner core, a solid sphere of metal. Just above that is the outer core, which is a layer of liquid metal. Above that is the mantle and on top of that sits the thin crust (fig. 1).

This will require a sizable amount of TNT to accomplish and some artistic skill to complete, but when finished, you will have a cool model of the Earth's interior all the way down to the core.

■ **GAME MODE**
Creative

■ **APPROXIMATE TIME TO COMPLETE**
2 hours

 FIND IT ONLINE
Do you know how many layers there are in Minecraft? At what level can you most likely find diamonds? What are the limits in a Minecraft world? The Minecraft Wiki is the perfect source for answers:
https://goo.gl/8A1VmN

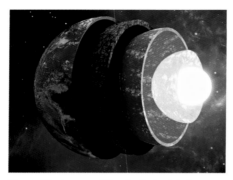

Fig. 1: The layers of the Earth in detail.

1. First, locate a relatively flat area in a grassland or mesa. You'll need a nice mixture of blocks to complete this design. You will be using TNT underground to create a large hole and you will want it to be somewhat spherical in shape. The bomb's dimensions from the bottom will be

   1 block on the bottom
   9 blocks (3 × 3) above the bottom layer
   25 blocks (5 × 5) above that layer
   49 blocks (7 × 7) in the middle
   25 blocks (5 × 5) above that layer
   9 blocks (3 × 3) above that layer
   1 block on top

   You will be building this below ground, but you may want to make a model above ground to practice (fig. 2).

2. Dig a hole 10 blocks deep and begin assembling your bomb by placing one block beneath your feet at the bottom of the hole. Next, hollow out a 9-square-block area just above the first block and fill it with TNT. As you climb up the mine shaft, first clear the area and then fill it with TNT (fig. 3). After finishing the top layer, fill the rest of the shaft as you fly out.

3. Using flint and steel, ignite the TNT and run. When you return, you should have a nice and deep—mostly spherical hole—portal to the core (fig. 4)!

4. The inner core of the Earth is solid, so just leave the exposed rock at the bottom alone. You'll need to add the outer core on top, but because that will be represented by lava, it should be the last thing you add. First, create a barrier for the outer core to keep the lava from flowing freely. We used orange concrete powder to represent the outer-core barrier (fig. 5). Don't destroy blocks, just place the orange blocks on top of the blocks already there to make several tall stacks.

GO BEYOND
The WorldEdit mod lets you make giant shapes, including spheres, using slash commands. Here's a quick video demonstration:
https://goo.gl/hXF1UX

Fig. 2: Arrange your TNT from the top using the pattern 1-9-25-49-25-9-1.

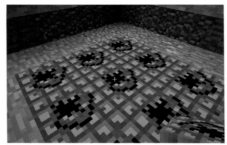
Fig. 3: Dig a shaft 10 blocks deep, start clearing each layer, and fill with TNT.

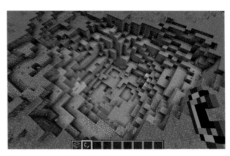
Fig. 4: The TNT will blow a deep, spherical hole in the ground.

Fig. 5: Use orange concrete powder for the outer core. Add lava as the inner core last.

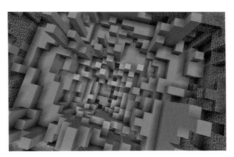
Fig. 6: The mantle is made from orange concrete and is larger than the inner core.

Fig. 7: Add a thin layer of blocks to represent the crust and surface of the Earth.

5. For the mantle, we used orange concrete. The mantle is larger than the outer core, so you will need to place more of it (fig. 6).

6. The crust is very thin compared to the other layers. Place a few blocks around the very edge to represent solid land, water, and vegetation (fig. 7). Finally, add a lava pool on top of the solid inner core at the bottom. Check out the image at the beginning of this lab.

7. You now have a giant representation of the layers of the Earth. What other features can you add to make it even more accurate?

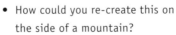

NOW TRY THIS
- How could you re-create this on the side of a mountain?
- Measure the approximate width of the hole you created. Double the size of your TNT bomb and place it 20 blocks deep instead of 10. When it explodes, does it make a hole twice the size?

SKETCHNOTE CHALLENGE
This lab should produce an incredible sketchnote with cutaway views of the Earth's layers and the horizon soil layers. Add a Minecraft twist!

In this activity, we'll create an electromagnet. We can use the electromagnet to learn about the relationship between electricity and magnetism as well as have fun creating magnetic fields to pick up items. Large electromagnets are used to pick up metal in junk yards, run electric motors, and scan our bodies using an MRI (magnetic resonance imaging) machine.

■ **APPROXIMATE TIME TO COMPLETE**
20 minutes

■ **MATERIALS**
Wire cutters
Coated wire
Sandpaper
Iron nail
AA battery
Gloves or electrical tape
Paper clips

 FIND IT ONLINE
Check out this great video on ferro fluid, a fluid that contains nanoparticles of magnetic material: *https://goo.gl/qCyjwH*

The Iron Age is an archaeological era that spanned hundreds of years. Once iron ore was discovered and smelted into useful iron tools and weapons, the world changed. Before the Iron Age, most civilizations used stone and wood tools, and some had bronze tools. Without the discovery and smelting of iron ore, we might not have magnets today.

We encounter magnets every day and likely don't fully understand how they work. It's almost like magic to see a magnet attract or repel another magnet or piece of iron. Magnets are in our headphones, cell phones, computers, microwaves, and even the strip on the back of a credit card.

Family Activity: Electromagnetism

1. Gather your materials. The wire used in this lab is called enameled copper, and it has a solid copper core with a very thin plastic-like coating.

2. With wire cutters, cut approximately 3 feet (1 m) of coated wire (fig. 1). Expose 1 inch (2.5 cm) from each end of the wire by stripping away the coating with sandpaper.

3. Tightly wrap the exposed wire around the iron nail, leave approximately 2 inches (5 cm) unwrapped on either end. Stop occasionally while wrapping the nail to tighten the wraps. The tighter and closer together the wraps are on the nail, the better the magnetic field (fig. 2).

4. Connect one AA battery between the two exposed ends of the wire. Because some of the electrical energy is converted into heat energy and might burn, wear gloves or wrap the electromagnet in electrical tape for safer handling. Try picking up paper clips and other metal items (fig. 3).

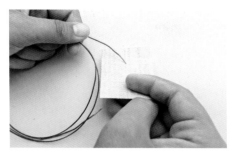

Fig. 1: You'll need about 3 feet (1 m) of wire to wrap around the nail. Use the sandpaper to expose the copper wire hidden below the outer coating.

Fig. 2: Wrap the wire around the nail until there is only 2 inches (5 cm) of wire left on each end to connect the battery. The tighter the wrap, the better the magnetic field.

Fig. 3: Place the battery between the wires. The electrical energy becomes a magnetic field and loses some energy in the form of heat. Take care when holding because it can get hot!

WHAT'S THE SCIENCE?

In this activity we created an electromagnet, a magnet created by a current of electrons. As the electrons flow, the magnetic field is created. The relationship between electricity and magnetism was discovered by Hans Christian Ørsted (1777–1851), now called Oersted's law. We can increase the magnetic field by increasing the current or by increasing the number of wire loops. Magnets have a north and south pole. Magnetic field lines point from the north to the south pole.

As common as magnets are, the way they work is quite complex. A magnetic field is made up of electrons moving around. Elements all around are made up of a nucleus with protons and electrons orbiting. Certain elements like iron, cobalt, and nickel have an unpaired electron orbiting. When a grouping of iron atoms are together with unpaired electrons orbiting, they create a magnetic field.

During the in-game section you'll relive the Iron Age in Minecraft. Without iron, there are no magnets. Imagine how radically different life would be moving from wood and stone tools and weapons to iron. The Iron Age was a massive technological advancement for cultures all around the world. Some cultures moved from stone to iron, while others experienced a Bronze Age. Bronze is a much softer metal, and it would be like having tools made only of gold in Minecraft. If you find diamond or gold while working through this lab, you can use those materials only to trade.

■ **GAME MODE**
Survival

■ **APPROXIMATE TIME TO COMPLETE**
2 hours

1. **Start with wood or stone tools as you mine to discover iron. You are on a mission to find iron and smelt it into tools and weapons to upgrade your kit and your world. It wasn't until after the Iron Age that people started experimenting with magnetism (fig. 1).**

2. **Once you have at least 7 iron ore, build a smelter house. Craft a furnace in a dedicated smelting area with plenty of ventilation. During the Iron Age, iron was smelted with different elements like carbon to make stronger tools. Smelters in ancient times were special buildings used solely for metal work (fig. 2).**

3. **With the iron ore smelted into iron ingots, start crafting new iron tools. A pickaxe is best at mining stone and ore, and a shovel is best at breaking dirt. Don't forget to craft a hoe! Every civilization needed to increase their ability to produce food to allow people to continue to mine and craft new items.**

Fig. 1: Try to find a quarry like the one pictured. This quarry had 7 blocks of iron ore! Too bad the iron ore isn't magnetic in the game.

Fig. 2: Smelters require extremely high heat. Incorporate your smelter into a hillside. Don't forget fuel for the furnace.

SKETCHNOTE CHALLENGE
Sketch a new iron tool in your science journal.

4. **Craft an anvil and repair your tools.** Before the Iron Age, you would have had to craft an entirely new tool out of stone, but now we can prolong the life of tools because of iron's malleability (fig. 3).

5. **Ready for iron armor?** Start with a helmet and boots because those are most like jewelry. Iron was used as a decoration before it was used as a full suit of armor. You'll need 5 iron ingots for the helmet and 4 more for boots (fig. 4).

6. **It's time to start using some of the experience points you've earned while mining, crafting, smelting iron, and protecting your home.** Craft bookshelves and place an enchanting table. You'll need to a couple diamonds, 4 obsidian, and a book to craft an enchanting table (fig. 5).

7. **You've just experienced the Iron Age!** Now get ready to make the leap into the Diamond Age. Just as it was a leap in technology to go from wood and stone to iron, it'll be another leap to diamond and enchanted items. Just as when you got your first stone tool or first iron tool, your first diamond tool becomes a major technological advancement.

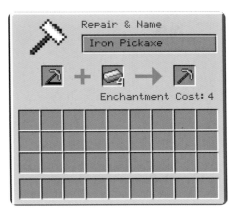

Fig. 3: Anvils are great not only for repairing damaged tools and weapons but also to name items. Name your tools and weapons so that if you drop them you can get them back.

Fig. 5: Enchantment tables are worth the all the time it takes mining to find the obsidian and diamond. Besides the floating glyphs from the bookshelves, make it an even cooler experience.

Fig. 4: Some of the first iron items were earrings and rings. Stretch your imagination to include a helmet and boots as decorative jewelry while mining for more iron ore.

NOW TRY THIS

- Try the /testforblock command to demonstrate an attraction.
- Research the first right-hand rule for electromagnets.
- Try using another metal, like aluminum, as the core for the electromagnet. What happened? Is the electromagnet stronger or weaker?

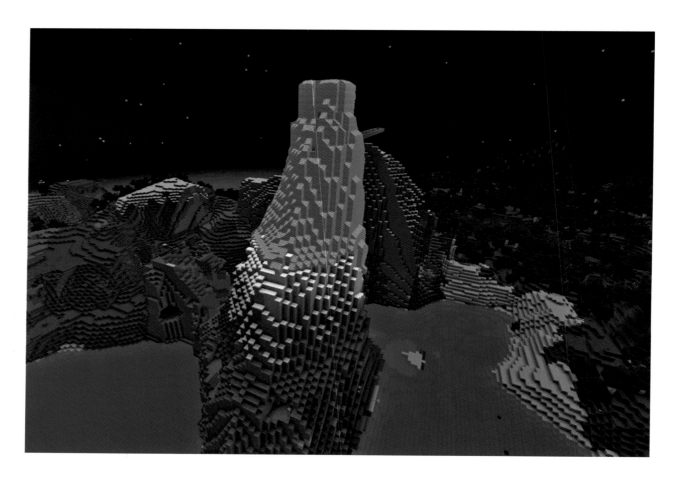

In this double volcano challenge, you'll build a volcano in and out of Minecraft. You'll use clay to make a mini version at home and redstone, lava, comparators, and repeaters to make a massive one in Minecraft.

 FIND IT ONLINE
If you're interested in volcanoes, visit one of our favorite sites, National Geographic Kids: *https://goo.gl/6T4TiL*

Family Activity: Erupting Volcano

Create a volcanic eruption using a plastic water bottle and a few common ingredients found around your home.

■ **APPROXIMATE TIME TO COMPLETE**

1 hour

■ **MATERIALS**

2 tablespoons (20 g) baking soda
1 squirt of liquid dish soap
2–3 drops each of red and yellow food coloring
1 small empty plastic bottle
Baking sheet or cake pan covered in plastic wrap for easy cleanup
Sand, clay, dirt, or papier-mâché to cover the bottle
2 tablespoons (30 ml) vinegar

1. **Gather your materials (fig. 1).**

2. **Add the baking soda, liquid dish soap, and food coloring to the bottle (fig. 2).**

3. **On the covered pan, build up your volcano around the plastic bottle. We used sand and modeling clay (fig. 3).**

4. **When ready, pour the vinegar into the bottle. The reaction creates carbon dioxide gas, which you will see as bubbles (fig. 4). It's called an endothermic reaction because it absorbs the surrounding air (energy), which goes into the reaction.**

Fig. 1: Ingredients include a small bottle, baking soda, vinegar, liquid dish soap, food coloring, and clay/sand.

Fig. 2: Add the baking soda, liquid dish soap, and food coloring to the bottle.

Fig. 3: Use materials such as sand, clay, dirt, or papier-mâché to create your volcano.

Fig. 4: Add the vinegar and enjoy the chemical reaction.

WHAT'S THE SCIENCE?

Volcanologists study volcanoes because they can get a peek into a very deep layer of the Earth. The further you travel beneath the Earth, the more intense the pressure. Eventually, you come to a point where the solid structure of rock breaks down and melts into material known as magma. Magma is less dense than the rock surrounding it, so it rises and will keep rising until denser material stops it. Eventually, the pressure of the magma can force the rock above it to break apart and the energy is released in the form of an explosive volcanic eruption.

You'll need to find a tall, slender mountain for this lab to work best. You'll be packing the mountaintop full of TNT and lava before connecting the cone to repeaters and a lever.

■ **GAME MODE**
Creative

■ **APPROXIMATE TIME TO COMPLETE**
2 hours

SKETCHNOTE CHALLENGE
Create a sketch of the layers of the volcano you created and compare them side-by-side with another sketch of a real volcano. How are they different and how are they similar?

1. Create the best lava fall possible by locating a tall, thin mountain near your lab (fig. 1).

2. Level the top of your mountain and dig a 6 × 7 hole. It can be larger, but make sure it is at least 7 blocks deep (fig. 2).

3. Fill the bottom three layers with lava and place one layer of stone on top of that to represent the Earth's crust (fig. 3).

4. Pack the remaining two layers with TNT. Be very careful not to get lava anywhere near the TNT or you'll be needing another mountain (fig. 4)!

5. Make the cone by covering the TNT with sand, and then add a short wall around the perimeter. Fill the container with lava (fig. 5).

6. Punch out a block on the side of the volcano, 4 blocks down, and locate a block of TNT. Connect redstone dust to the TNT block and run it back to a lever, but do not connect it to the lever yet (fig. 6).

Fig. 1: Volcanoes are usually cone shaped; you'll need to find one like this near your camp.

Fig. 2: Create a magma chamber that's at least 7 blocks deep.

7. Add several repeaters to the redstone circuit coming from the exposed block of TNT. Set each to three clicks to slow down the ignition of the TNT and allow you time to get a better view.

8. When ready, connect the redstone circuit coming from the TNT to your lever. As the Moon rises in the distance, pull the lever and watch the massive explosion (fig. 7). Following that, lava will pour from the new crater down to the ground.

9. As a bonus, use the information you learned in Lab 12 and set off a fire charge show just before the explosion.

Fig. 3: Add lava until the bottom three layers are covered, then top with one layer of stone.

Fig. 4: Fill in the top with TNT.

Fig. 5: Cover the TNT with a layer of sand, add a short wall around the exterior, and top it off with more lava.

Fig. 6: Carefully attach redstone to the TNT and run it down and away from the volcano. To be safe, do not attach the other end.

GO BEYOND

Is it possible to create a volcano that erupts each night at sunset using pistons, lava, and solar sensors? What kind of mechanisms would you need to refill the magma chamber?

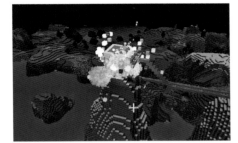

Fig. 7: Attach the lever, pull, and fly away to get a good view. You can also include fire charges in the setup. See Lab 12 (page 76) for details.

NOW TRY THIS

- The magma chamber can go down much deeper, but you will need to add some TNT in spots to open more vents.
- How could you make a volcano using pistons that would allow lava to flow on command?

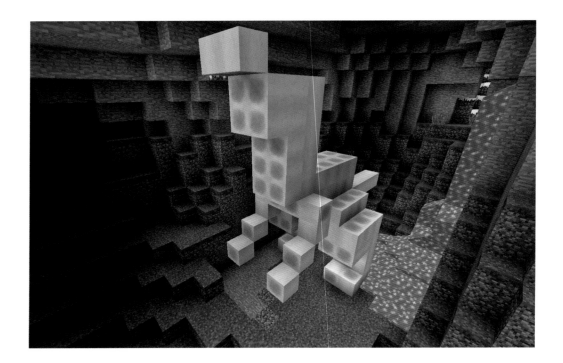

Put on your hats because it's time to explore life as a paleontologist. In Minecraft, you'll be creating a dinosaur dig site while unearthing ancient fossils. Outside the game, you will also be conducting a dig while trying to piece a dinosaur back together.

WHAT'S THE SCIENCE?

Dinosaur fossils form when a dinosaur dies, or becomes trapped in mud or very sandy water and is quickly covered by more mud or other substances like tar or ice. Minerals seep into the bones and harden them, turning them into fossils. Scientists discover fossils when the ancient material that entrapped them wears away and exposes the mineralized bones.

Family Activity: Dinosaur Dig

You may be familiar with the reaction and result of adding the right amount of water to cornstarch. It produces a gooey substance referred to as Oobleck. In this lab, you'll bury dinosaur parts in Oobleck and let it dry. The next day, break it open and try to reassemble the dinosaur.

■ **APPROXIMATE TIME TO COMPLETE**

30 minutes + 1 day of drying time

■ **MATERIALS**

A shatterproof container to hold the mixture

About 2 cups (280 g) cornstarch

About 1 cup (235 ml) water

Mixing bowl

Stirring stick

2 or 3 small plastic dinosaur toys, cut into pieces

Hammer and safety goggles

Fig. 1: A mixture of cornstarch and water plus dinosaur toys equals a paleontological dig.

Fig. 2: Place the dinosaur pieces throughout the mixture.

Fig. 3: Submerge the toy pieces completely and allow the mixture to dry.

Fig. 4: Carefully fracture the surface and then you can begin the excavation.

1. Gather your materials (fig. 1). Depending on the size of your shatterproof container, mix together approximately 2 parts cornstarch to 1 part water in a bowl. Stir to combine. You are looking for a liquid with the consistency of thick paint or honey.

2. Pour approximately half the mixture into your container. Scatter the dinosaur pieces throughout the mixture (fig. 2). Gently pour the remaining mixture into the container to cover the dinosaurs completely (fig. 3).

3. Place in sunlight or other dry location. The mixture will dry and become semihard as it returns to a solid form. Lightly tap or scrape it with a hammer or heavy spoon to crack open and search for the dinosaur pieces (fig. 4).

With the release of Minecraft 1.10 for the PC, a fun new structure block was added. With a bone block, players can create giant fossilized creatures. To encourage young paleontologists, fossils now appear underground and take one of twelve different forms. In this challenge, multiple players will use bone block to make fossil dinosaurs of their own and then quickly encase them in stone for each other to uncover.

■ **GAME MODE**
Creative

■ **APPROXIMATE TIME TO COMPLETE**
2 hours

Fig. 1: We found an empty cave, the perfect spot for a giant velociraptor made from bone blocks.

SKETCHNOTE CHALLENGE
Have everyone sketch and label their dinosaur in your lab book. Make sure they sign it, too. How might you combine several dinosaurs to make one? What would it look like if you took the coolest features of each? What would you call it?

1. Each player should create a fossil based on a real dinosaur. With the other players, visit ewdinosaurs.com, select several dinosaurs, and write each name on a small piece of paper. Fold the paper, mix them up, and have everyone select one randomly.

2. Players build their dinosaur in a location where they cannot be seen by the others. A big cave works well, as does a deep pit or canyon (fig. 1). Build your dinosaur using bone. Check out our velociraptor at the beginning of this lab.

FIND IT ONLINE
To learn more about Minecraft fossils, visit the Minecraft Wiki: *https://goo.gl/JFua7Z*

3. To quickly cover your skeleton in stone, grab a lava bucket. Start at the top, and pour the lava out so that it covers your fossil. The bone block will not be destroyed by the lava (fig. 2).

4. When water encounters lava, it turns the lava into either cobblestone or obsidian. Grab a bucket of water and pour it on top of the lava in several places (fig. 3).

5. Now that the lava has turned into rock, get rid of the water by right-clicking with an empty bucket. Find all the blocks you poured water on originally and collect it with the empty bucket (fig. 4).

6. How does it look? Need another layer of rock? If so, repeat steps 3–5.

7. When everyone has finished, it's time to dig out each other's fossil and see if you can identify it.

Fig. 2: Pour lava on top of your dinosaur to create lava falls.

Fig. 3: When water mixes with lava, it cools the lava and creates stone.

Fig. 4: Collect all the water with an empty bucket.

NOW TRY THIS

- Instead of designing their own fossils, more advanced players could use the game command /gamemode 3, which will place them in spectator mode. With this, they can have a fossil hunt of their own by flying beneath the surface.

- There are twelve types of fossils that can be found beneath swamps and deserts. Who can find and excavate the most in 1 hour? Type /gamemode 1 to return to creative mode.

GO BEYOND

Are you interested in finding Minecraft fossils underground, but you don't know where to look? YouTuber OMGchad has some great tips. You'll need to use the command /gamemode 3 to be able to find them. It also helps to drink a night-vision potion before switching game modes to see things more clearly. He has all the details in a video: *https://goo.gl/Qyw1YW*

Cycles in Science

To complete this quest, Minecrafters and their families
will explore cycles in science.

One thing you've got to love about Minecraft: chickens! Any Minecraft player will tell you that chickens are a wonderful source of meat and eggs, but my goodness—they can be so annoying. We decided to give them their own spotlight in this lab. You'll learn how to automate an egg ranch in Minecraft and participate in a fun engineering competition with family and friends.

WHAT'S THE SCIENCE?

Look in your refrigerator or at a package that a delivery driver brings you and see how the product is packaged. What materials or precautions did the shipper or manufacturer include to keep the product safe or fresh? Scientists help develop inexpensive, lightweight, and recyclable packaging materials that will allow even the most fragile of objects to be shipped around the world with the smallest amount of waste. Egg containers are usually made from cardboard or a foam-like material. Why do you think that is?

Family Activity: Egg Drop Challenge

The egg drop challenge is upon you. There are several options for completing this lab, so select the one that works best for you. The goal of each is to engineer a container that will keep an egg from breaking, despite being dropped from a predetermined height.

■ **APPROXIMATE TIME TO COMPLETE**

1 hour

■ **MATERIALS**

Eggs

Utility tape

Containers

Various packing material

You will also need a location, such as a second-story balcony, from which to drop your containers. If that is not possible, each container can be tossed or launched into the air from ground level.

Fig. 1: Search the house for materials and look for items that can be recycled after this lab is over.

Fig. 2: Who can create a container that saves an egg and costs the least?

Option 1: Materials

With this option, limit all engineers to the same set of materials (fig. 1). Engineers can use only the materials given, but may assemble their package in any way they wish.

Option 2: Containers

Give each participant the same container, such as take-out boxes, Styrofoam cups, or recyclable plant containers, but let them choose packing materials from a large pile of options. Another variation of this option is to toss a "secret ingredient" into the mix, something that everyone must use.

Option 3: Math Game

Each item used has a value, or imaginary cost, associated with it. The goal is to see who can keep an egg safe at the lowest cost of materials (fig. 2). Items like bubble wrap and cotton should cost much more than tape.

Option 4: Mass

If you have access to a digital scale, you will be able to determine the mass of each container. Mass indicates the amount of matter in the container. Who can design a container that has the lowest mass and keeps an egg from breaking?

Option 5: Size

What is the smallest container you can design to save the egg? Use a measuring tape around the widest location to determine a winner.

What would you do with all the cake and pumpkin pie you could eat? Well, you'll need dozens of eggs, so let's get busy building a chicken coop that collects eggs for you automatically. Build it near your laboratory, but not too near because these chickens will be making a lot of noise!

■ **GAME MODE**
Creative or survival

■ **APPROXIMATE TIME TO COMPLETE**
1 hour

FIND IT ONLINE
• Of course, chickens are a good source of meat, as well. Check out this redstone-powered automated chicken farm: *https://goo.gl/apD1Fi*

SKETCHNOTE CHALLENGE
We've used hoppers here as a collector, but hoppers can behave differently. Research them on the Minecraft Wiki and then sketch a diagram of how hoppers works.

1. **Build a 7 × 7 foundation slab using the block of your choice (fig. 1).**
2. **Build an exterior wall all the way around, leaving a spot for a door. Attach 6 hoppers to the back of 6 trapped chests (fig. 2).**

Fig. 1: Start with a 7 × 7 foundation somewhere near your lab.

Fig. 2: Add hoppers and trapped chests, as shown.

Fig. 3: You'll need to right-click on the trapped chest with the hopper in your hand to attach it.

Fig. 4: Add bars and walls before placing chickens.

Fig. 5: Snug as chickens in a coop.

3. To attach a hopper to the back of a trapped chest, hold down the shift key while right-clicking with the hopper in your hand (fig. 3).

4. Extend the walls to the inside and add iron bars across the length of both sides of the coop (fig. 4).

5. With a chicken spawn egg (or regular egg) in your hand, right-click inside the hopper to place a chicken in it. Quickly place one more wood plank block on the roof to trap the chicken inside (fig. 5).

6. Check each morning and you should discover a fresh supply of eggs inside the chests.

GO BEYOND
Flowing water is often used in designs that emphasize automated collection. Here is one that includes a giant chicken swimming pool feeding eggs into a vast network of hoppers. Notice how the hoppers all spill into one chest. Check it out here: *https://goo.gl/TiJvFe*

NOW TRY THIS
- Need a lot of eggs? See how many chickens you can get into each hopper.
- Now that you've automated egg collection, design a way to harvest wheat.
- Create an entire working farm filled with animals and vegetables.

Build a Battery

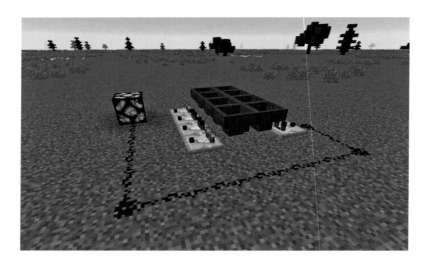

Batteries are easy to build! Using common household items, we can create a steady supply of electrical energy. In this lab, we'll build a small expandable battery out of coins, foil, and cardboard. After building this simple battery, you may just have a newfound appreciation for batteries you encounter daily.

■ **APPROXIMATE TIME TO COMPLETE**
30 minutes

■ **MATERIALS**
Pennies
Pencil
Cardboard from a cereal or tissue box
Scissors
Foil
Bowl
White vinegar
Tape
Small LED or multimeter

Batteries are used in nearly all the electronic equipment we interact with daily. From cell phones to video game controllers, batteries have the important job of supplying portable electricity. Batteries supply electricity through a chemical reaction that creates electrical energy. By recharging rechargeable batteries, we reverse the process to resupply electrical energy.

For the in-game section of the lab, you'll build a hopper pipe that simulates the flow of electrons within a battery. In the family activity, you'll build a battery with some pennies, foil, cardboard, and vinegar. Increase the voltage of your battery by adding more layers (cells).

 FIND IT ONLINE
Northwestern University has a great resource on how a battery works: *https://goo.gl/ez1fQ*

GO BEYOND
What happens when you add or take away cells of your battery? What other materials can you use to make a battery? How can you make your hopper pipe move faster?

Family Activity: Build a Battery

1. Gather your materials. You'll need coin-size circles of cardboard. Trace one of the pennies on the cardboard at least 10 times (fig. 1). Cut them out carefully, too large and the edges of the cardboard will make the battery less efficient.

2. This battery uses the chemical properties of dissimilar metals to transfer energy. In addition to copper, the battery uses aluminum foil. You'll need about 10 pieces of foil. Fold the foil 4 times. Trace a coin and cut out the shapes (fig. 2). Carefully separate the foil layers.

3. Place the 10 pieces of cardboard into a small bowl. Pour enough white vinegar to cover each cardboard piece. Allow the cardboard to absorb the vinegar; this may take over a minute (fig. 3).

(continued)

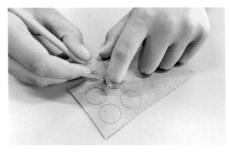

Fig. 1: Trace the coin on the cardboard to create a template for cutting. You'll find this thin cardboard in cereal and tissue boxes.

Fig. 2: Allow the cardboard to soak in the vinegar. The cardboard needs time to absorb the liquid to allow the electrons to pass through the cells.

Fig. 3: Folding the foil allows us to make one cut. Once the foil is cut, take care when separating the thin layers. *Tip:* Wet one fingertip to grab each thin layer of foil.

NOW TRY THIS

Explore rechargeable batteries with solar power. A small solar-powered garden light is a great place to start.

SKETCHNOTE CHALLENGE

Sketch the details of your copper coin, foil, and cardboard battery.

4. Stack your battery in this order: coin, foil, vinegar-soaked cardboard, coin, foil, vinegar-soaked cardboard (fig. 4). Stack at least 8 layers. Begin and end the battery with a coin. Wrap tape around the stacked battery to help it stay together.

5. Connect a small LED or multimeter to your battery to measure the voltage (fig. 5). If the voltage seems especially low, check the connections between the layers. AA and AAA batteries produce 1.5 volts, and a 9-volt battery produces 9 volts.

Fig. 4: Start and end your battery with a coin. Layer the battery: coin, foil, cardboard. Each layer is a battery cell. Add more cells to add more energy.

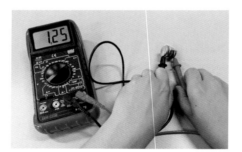

Fig. 5: Attach a multimeter or small LED light to measure how much electrical energy your battery is producing. Play with the lineup of the cells to improve efficiency.

WHAT'S THE SCIENCE?

The battery you created has three parts: an anode, a cathode, and the electrolyte. Each three-part layer—coin, foil, cardboard—makes one battery cell. The positive terminal is the cathode, while the negative is the anode, and the electrolyte allows the chemical reaction inside the battery to initiate the flow of electrons to travel from anode (negative) to cathode (positive). The anode releases the electron while the cathode accepts the electron. Once the battery is connected with some resistance, like a lightbulb or the multimeter, the circuit is closed. As the electrons flow around the circuit, the light illuminates or the multimeter displays the energy produced. The design of your battery is built on the Voltaic pile battery by Alessandro Volta (1745–1827), which he devised in 1800. The copper and aluminum pieces are electrodes while the vinegar is the electrolyte. The electrolyte increases conductivity, which increases your battery's voltage.

Hoppers are clever items to help automate your work. When we drop an item into one of the hoppers, it is transferred like the chemicals in a physical battery around a circuit.

■ **GAME MODE**
Creative

■ **APPROXIMATE TIME TO COMPLETE**
25 minutes

1. Craft or collect at least 8 hoppers, 8 redstone comparators, and an item of your choice.

2. Place the first hopper in a space with room for 7 more. The consecutive hoppers must be attached to the first by holding shift on the PC. The hopper pipe must be like a circuit with one hopper connected to the next (fig. 1).

3. Break the first hopper and replace it by holding shift and your place button. This will make a complete circuit and determine whether the hopper pipe continues circulating the item (fig. 2).

Fig. 1: Notice the bottom of the hopper makes a 90-degree turn toward the connected hopper. This connected hopper section is what allows the items to travel between the hoppers.

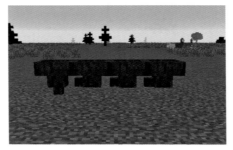

Fig. 2: The first hopper acts as a placeholder to attach hoppers 2 through 7.

4. Stand on top of the hopper and place a comparator pointing away from the hopper. The comparators will become a visual to see what happens as the item travels around the circuit. Drop any item into one of the hoppers. Watch it move from one hopper to the next, lighting a comparator as it circulates (fig. 3).

5. If your item doesn't circulate, go back to steps 2 and 3 to make sure your hoppers are connected in the pipe form. The lower part of the hopper must be curved.

6. For added visual effect, place redstone dust and a lamp down from one end of your hopper pipe to the other. Although this isn't improving your hopper pipe, it appears to look more like a complete circuit with battery, wires, and light (see photo page 104).

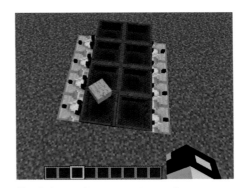

Fig. 3: Leave the comparators as item indicators or connect them with redstone dust to operate a redstone-powered item. Pistons also make great visuals.

NOW TRY THIS

- Your hopper pipe is a slow redstone clock. Try adding it to your chain reaction contraption in Lab 22 (page 122).

- This build would work great with the Zombie Dance Party lab in our first book, *Unofficial Minecraft Lab for Kids.*

Create an Ecosystem

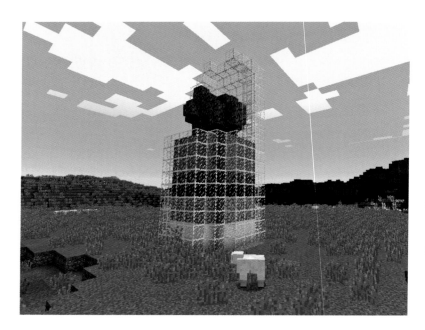

Terrariums allow the opportunity to grow plants in different climates. If you live in a dry, desert-like climate, you can grow humidity-loving tropical plants in a closed terrarium, which creates its own environment that is more humid than the ambient air in your house.

In the hands-on activity, you'll create a closed terrarium that not only nourishes plants with nutrients from soil but also recycles water through the water cycle. In the game activity, you'll replicate a terrarium near your science laboratory.

GO BEYOND
If you love plants, look into becoming a horticulturist or landscape architect.

Tropical plants like ferns, fittonia, baby's tears, pilea, begonia, cryptanthus, oak leaf creeping fig, and small palm trees work great in a closed terrarium. Terrariums make great gifts because they require little care and look great. Building one with a large clear and empty soda bottle is a great way to upcycle. Take care when adding the layers to your terrarium.

■ **APPROXIMATE TIME TO COMPLETE**
   45 minutes

■ **MATERIALS**
   Rubber band
   Plastic drink bottle (2L)
   Ruler
   Marker
   Scissors
   Sand
   Small rocks
   Activated charcoal
   Sphagnum moss
   Potting soil
   Small moisture-loving plant of your
      choice (see suggestions above)
   Clear packing tape

1. Gather the materials (fig. 1).

2. Stretch a rubber band around the bottle about 4 inches (10 cm) above the bottom. Draw a line on the bottle above the band (fig. 2). Remove the rubber band and cut along line.

Family Activity: Terrarium

Fig. 1: Assemble your materials.

Fig. 2: Trace a rubber band before cutting.

3. Layer 1 inch (2.5 cm) of sand, 1 inch (2.5 cm) of small rocks, and a ½ inch (1.3 cm) of activated charcoal (fig. 3). The charcoal has tiny openings that grab impurities in the water, like a water filter you might use at home.

4. Add a thin layer of moist sphagnum moss, and 2 inches (5 cm) of damp potting soil (wet the moss and potting soil before adding them to the terrarium). Add your small plant (fig. 4).

5. Place the upper section of the bottle on top. Use tape to seal (fig. 5). Twist off the cap to add water or allow excess water to evaporate. Learn from our mistake: too much light will burn the plants.

WHAT'S THE SCIENCE?

A closed terrarium creates a humid, self-watering environment ideal for moisture-loving plants. The clear plastic bottle allows heat and light to enter and traps the water. Because the bottle is closed, the water cycle is simulated. As the water heats up, it evaporates and condenses on the interior walls of the bottle. The terrarium is layered with different materials to allow excess water to drain through the soil, preventing root rot through swampy soil. The water at the bottom of the bottle is then ready to evaporate and condense on the walls near the plant leaves. Although plants use photosynthesis to make their food, they need the soil to absorb nutrients like nitrogen, phosphorus, and potassium.

Fig. 3: Layer sand, small rocks, and activated charcoal in the bottom.

Fig. 4: Add moss, moist potting soil, and the plant. Add a critter for decoration.

Fig. 5: Tape the top section of the plastic bottle with clear packing tape.

In this lab, you'll get to craft a terrarium near your science laboratory. The family activity is about creating a closed terrarium that is beneficial for tropical plants. In this part of the lab, you'll craft a Minecraft version of a closed terrarium to simulate the family activity. Come up with your own enclosure shape, such as a large bottle or even a sphere.

The Jungle biome is most closely related to a real-life humid environment. Inside the Minecraft terrarium, create a small version of the Jungle biome. Build the terrarium above ground using clear glass blocks and the layers of soil to replicate a real terrarium in life.

■ **GAME MODE**
Creative

■ **APPROXIMATE TIME TO COMPLETE**
25 minutes

 FIND IT ONLINE
Try playing Terraria—it's like a 2D version of Minecraft that's in a massive terrarium:
https://terraria.org

PLANTS	MOBS	
Tall grass	**Passive Mobs:**	**Hostile Mobs:**
Vines	Ocelots	Spiders
Ferns	Chickens	Enderman
Jungle wood and leaves	Cows	Witches
Oak wood and leaves	Sheep	Skeletons
Dandelion flowers	Pigs	Creepers
Cocoa beans	Parrots	Zombies
Poppy flowers	Villagers	
Melons		

1. Select a location near your science laboratory or field station. Build your terrarium in a biome that is drier than the Jungle biome to provide a contrast between dry and humid environments.

2. Plan your bottle shape. Build a 6 × 6 base layer of glass with cobblestone surrounding it. Break the corner blocks to make the base look like a rounded bottle shape (fig. 1).

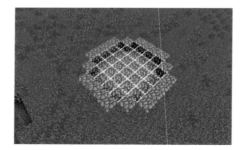

Fig. 1: Start your bottle shape with a layer of cobblestone for added visual support. Break the corners of the 6 × 6 shape to make a rounded look, just like the bottle you used in the family activity portion.

3. Build the lower half of the terrarium by crafting 9 levels of glass following your base layer pattern. Leave a side section exposed for greater access to the layers of soil (fig. 2).

4. The base layer of the terrarium needs to be sand. On top of the sand, add a layer of cobblestone. Both the stone and the sand act as filters for the water as it drains through the soil. On top of the cobblestone, add a layer of coal blocks. Just like in our family activity, the coal acts like a scrubber for the water, adding greater purification as it is recycled in the terrarium (fig. 3).

5. Add one layer of jungle leaves to simulate sphagnum moss. The moss adds a layer of moisture to help your plant self-water. Add dirt blocks to fill in the top three layers.

6. Build a jungle tree out of jungle wood and leaf blocks to simulate a growing tree. Jungle saplings will only grow if you have a terrarium with plenty of room. If you want to grow plants from seeds, try adding smaller plants found in the Jungle biome like melons, ferns, and flowers (fig. 4).

7. Craft the top section of the terrarium to resemble a bottle. Double the base 9 layers to craft the top half of the bottle, depending on the types of plants planted. Add a cap at the top to make it more visually similar to a bottle (fig. 5).

NOW TRY THIS

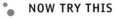

Connect your terrarium with your science laboratory, but be sure to set up a method of sealing your terrarium to keep the water cycle in a closed loop.

Fig. 2: Build the lower half of the terrarium bottle. Leave a side section exposed as you build for easy access to the layers of soil.

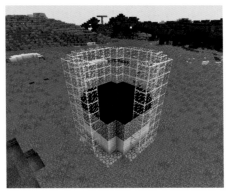

Fig. 3: The lower three layers are all about purifying and collecting the water as it drains inside the terrarium. This is similar to how water is purified in real life as it leaches through layers of earth to the water table below.

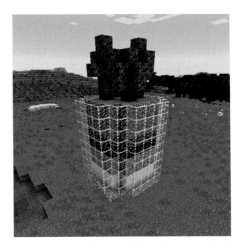

Fig. 4: To save time, craft jungle trees out of jungle wood and leaves. Try planting jungle saplings; they may work only if you crafted a large terrarium.

Fig. 5: To complete the closed terrarium, craft the top section of the bottle. Use red wool or concrete to give that just-capped look. Consider adding a couple of passive mobs inside your terrarium.

Quantum Physics

It's time to think about the very small and learn how scientists believe information is transported across great distances very quickly. You'll begin by examining 3D movie glasses, up close, and uncover how our brain makes sense of what we see. In Minecraft, you'll learn about the science around a concept known as quantum teleportation. You'll use command blocks to set up teleport stations that allow digital visitors to move quickly around your STEM world.

FIND IT ONLINE

You can view images of what the surface of Mars looks like by visiting the NASA site, below, and wearing your 3D glasses. How do you think the robot was able to take these photos? *https://goo.gl/8C4JWm*

Family Activity: Shifting Perspectives

In this lab, you will look at the world through 3D movie glasses, learn how a stereoscopic image is formed, and examine the role color plays in our lives.

- **APPROXIMATE TIME TO COMPLETE**

    1 hour

- **MATERIALS**

    Red-and-blue 3D glasses, one for each family member, plus one additional pair

    A mirror

    Scissors

1. Gather your materials (fig. 1). All participants put on their glasses and face each other or look in the mirror. What do you notice with both eyes open about the other person? Now close one eye, then open it and close the other. What happens?

2. Cut one pair in half and cut off the part that goes around the ear (fig. 2). Lay one color on top of the other and look through the lens. What do you notice? Look up at the sky, but away from the Sun. What color is the sky? Can you explain why?

3. Look at figure 3. It looks like an out-of-focus image of the planet Mars. Put on your 3D glasses and you'll see a 3D image of the red planet. Other *anaglyphs* can be found online.

Fig. 1: You can find 3D red/blue glasses at novelty stores and online.

Fig. 2: Separate each color with scissors.

Fig. 3: View this anaglyph with your 3D glasses on.

WHAT'S THE SCIENCE?

Our eyes gather information transmitted by light and our brain interprets it. Photons are the smallest unit of light and the information they transport is sometimes referred to as *quanta*. Red-and-blue glasses process two images taken by two different cameras slightly apart (just like our eyes) and merge them together to trick our brain. One camera has a blue filter on it and the other, a red filter. The result is a 3D effect as our brain attempts to make sense of the transmitted information and, as a result, we experience an awareness of depth.

You designed and built a cool, automated laboratory in Lab 1 and have since created many additional field stations where you've been hard at work. Let's make it easier for your character to get to each work site by setting up command block teleporters.

In the world of physics, many scientists believe that information, like the exact location of your Minecraft character, can be transported over great distances very quickly. It's time to test that idea in Minecraft.

■ **GAME MODE**
Creative

■ **APPROXIMATE TIME TO COMPLETE**
2 hours

1. **Command blocks cannot be found in the regular inventory, so players must summon one by typing in a command. For this to work, set the game settings to allow cheats, and you must play in creative mode. Type in the following command to summon a command block:**

/give @p minecraft:command_block

A command block like this one should pop into your inventory (fig. 1).

2. **You will need to visit each of your field stations, stand in a comfortable spot, and record the coordinates. Begin with your science lab. Create a table like the one below to record the x, y, and z coordinates at each site. When you are standing in the correct location, press the F3 key and look for the three numbers just after XYZ. They may look something like -2430 78 432.**

3. **Once you have all the coordinates you need, it's time to create your teleporter. Determine where you wish to place it in your lab. You will need as many command blocks as you have research stations. We placed our command blocks in the floor (fig. 2).**

4. **Right-click on top of each command block. In the box just below "Console Command," type the following:**

/tp @p x y z

Replace the x, y, and z with the coordinates of the field station you wish to visit using this command block. Be sure to add a space after each coordinate. Click Done when you are finished.

GO BEYOND

There are two more versions in addition to command blocks. Chain command and repeating command blocks are set up in a similar way, but each can control a different aspect of the game. Visit the Minecraft Wiki and read about each block, then add one of each to your science lab: *https://goo.gl/LryCxv*

	Home Base	Desert Field Station	Mountain Field Station	Ocean Field Station	Polar Field Station
X					
Y					
Z					

5. Grab a button from your inventory and, while holding down the shift key, right-click on top of the command block to place it on the block (fig. 3). Your first command block teleporter is now ready to test! Click the button to see if you are transported to the field station.

6. Now that you are at your first field station, place another command block near the spot you just landed on. This time, dig a hole and place the command block inside. Right-click it and add the coordinates of your lab home base. Instead of a button, place a pressure plate on top of the command block by holding down the shift key before right-clicking (fig. 4).

7. Finish up by repeating steps 4–6 for each field station you wish to connect to your teleporter. To wrap it up and make it easier to identify each teleporter, place a sign behind each command block and type the name of the field station destination.

Fig. 1: Summon a command block by typing /give @p minecraft:command_block.

Fig. 2: Place your command blocks near each other, one for each field station you wish to visit.

Fig. 3: Place a button on top of a command block by holding down the shift key and then right-clicking.

Fig. 4: By adding a pressure plate, visitors can step on top of the command block and be transported back to your lab.

NOW TRY THIS
- Create teleporters using levers or pressure plates.
- Can you build a teleporter that appears invisible?

SKETCHNOTE CHALLENGE
This is the perfect opportunity to sketch a map of your world. What icons would you use to represent each field station? Also, sketch something that reminds you about what kinds of science take place there.

FIND IT ONLINE
Did you have fun typing code into your command blocks? There are many more commands that can be issued with command blocks based on the version of the game you are playing. Try out the latest commands for each version by visiting the DigMinecraft site: *https://goo.gl/hYMgjn*

QUEST 6

Engineering Challenge

To complete this quest, Minecrafters and their families
will engineer solutions to several design challenges.

In this activity, you'll create a simple program so your partner can complete the dot programming game. A program is a list of instructions; this one tells your partner how to move through the game. The goal is to successfully move your partner through dot by dot, without running into any boundary lines. We created four designs that start off easy and gradually increase in difficulty.

■ **APPROXIMATE TIME TO COMPLETE**
  1 hour

■ **MATERIALS**
  Dot programming sheet (see page 135)
  Pencil
  Paper

Programming has become increasingly important in our world. It takes programming to build and more programming to update Minecraft. Learn about programming while playing Minecraft!

1. **To complete the game, your partner will follow your instructions (program) to connect the dots. From the start position, write each move your partner will need to make from dot to dot. Choose from the following moves: draw right, draw left, draw up, draw down. If you'd like your partner to move in any direction more than one dot, you'll need to tell them. For example, to move up 4 dots, your program would read, "Draw up × 4" (fig. 1).**

DRAW UP 8
DRAW RIGHT 7
DRAW UP 8
DRAW RIGHT 6
DRAW DOWN 14
DRAW LEFT 6

Fig. 1: Write commands like these for your game partner. The commands tell your partner where to draw the lines.

2. **The completed list of moves (commands) is your program. Give your program to your game partner and ask them to follow your moves exactly, even if it means not following the game boundary lines on the sheet. If your program crosses the game boundary lines or over itself, it's buggy. Debug your program by altering the moves (fig. 2).**

3. **You can create a program for one of the shapes shown in figure 3, or draw your own design on dot paper (see page 135) and craft a program for your partner to follow.**

Fig. 2: Instead of following the boundary lines, your partner should follow the commands to connect the dots.

Fig. 3: Four sample dot-programming templates you can use.

WHAT'S THE SCIENCE?

Programming is the act of creating instructions in a specific language that a computer can compile and use. Computer science covers more than just programming; at its core, computer science is about solving problems. Computer scientists often become software engineers, people who work to build and repair software code.

FIND IT ONLINE

- This video produced by Facebook explains the concept of computer science: *https://goo.gl/IoT1JO*
- Go to this web address for a printable version of our sample dot programming template *https://goo.gl/7eKGME*

For this in-game part of the lab, you'll type commands and get items that are impossible to collect in game. Who doesn't want enchanted weapons with the 32747 level? There are many more commands you can try in game that are not covered in this lab. Try to figure out how to customize the commands as you work through the lab.

■ **GAME MODE**

Creative or survival (must be OP)

■ **APPROXIMATE TIME TO COMPLETE**

1 hour

FIND IT ONLINE

- For a list of all the commands and how to use them, visit the Minecraft Wiki: *https://goo.gl/UKwyRP*
- Devise even crazier commands using the MCStacker website: *https://mcstacker.bimbimma.com*
- Subscribe to Jragon014 to learn how to make your own Minecraft commands: *https://goo.gl/zl67WA*

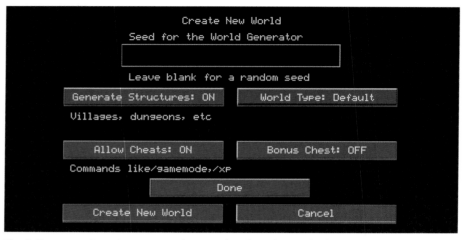

Fig. 1: You must allow cheats to run /commands. It's easiest to do this before creating the world, but if you're already in a world and didn't allow cheats, then open the world to LAN.

1. **You must be OP (operator) in the world. In single player, either start the world with cheats on or open your world to LAN, press Escape, and you'll see a button that says open to LAN. The commands must be typed in the chat box by pressing t or / to start a command (fig. 1).**

2. **Start with altering the weather and time of day. Type /weather thunder 100 and press Enter. Type /set time night and press Enter. There are three weather options: clear, rain, and thunder. The number at the end of the weather command is the number of seconds you're changing the weather.**

3. **Commands can be location specific. One of the most useful commands is the /tp command to teleport users around the world. Type /tp with coordinates to teleport yourself to a new location (fig. 2). An example is /tp 100 75 -270. When playing with others, teleport to them by typing /tp (person being teleported) (person at location). An example is /tp cscottsy escottsy (this command will send cscottsy to escottsy). For more on coordinates, review Lab 5.**

4. **Many of the features you're used to are controlled by the command / gamerule. Try to turn pvp on by typing /gamerule pvp true (or false to turn it off).**

Fig. 2: Teleport anywhere in the world and to other players using the simple /tp command.

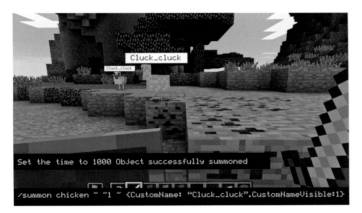

Fig. 3: We summoned a chicken with a visible name, named Cluck_cluck one block above our coordinates.

5. With the /summon command, things get interesting. You can summon much more than a regular creeper or cow. With a few additions to a command or argument, you can change their characteristics. Type /summon and then press the tab key to see a list of options. An example is /summon chicken ~ ~1 ~ {CustomName:"Cluck_cluck",CustomNameVisible:1} (fig. 3).

6. Super enchant a diamond sword by typing /give @p minecraft:diamond_sword 1 0 {ench:[{id:16,lvl:32767},{id:21,lvl:32767},{id:20,lvl:32767}]}. This command will give you a diamond sword with Sharpness (16), Looting (21), and Fire Aspect (20) at a maximum level of 32767 (fig. 4).

PE	PC	ARMOR
0	0	Protection
1	1	Fire Protection
2	2	Feather Falling
3	3	Blast Protection
4	4	Projectile Protection
5	6	Respiration
6	8	Aqua Affinity
7	5	Thorns
8	7	Depth Strider
9	25	Frost Walker
PE	**PC**	**WEAPONS**
16	9	Sharpness
17	10	Smite
18	11	Bane of Arthropods
19	12	Knockback
20	13	Fire Aspect
21	14	Looting
PE	**PC**	**TOOLS**
32	15	Efficiency
33	16	Silk Touch
34	17	Unbreaking (works for all)
35	18	Fortune
PE	**PC**	**BOW**
48	19	Power
49	20	Punch
50	21	Flame
51	22	Infinity
PE	**PC**	**FISHING ROD**
61	23	Luck of the Sea
62	24	Lure
70	26	Mending (works for all)

Fig. 4: Use this table as you craft your own enchanted tools. Don't forget to share super-powerful items with your friends.

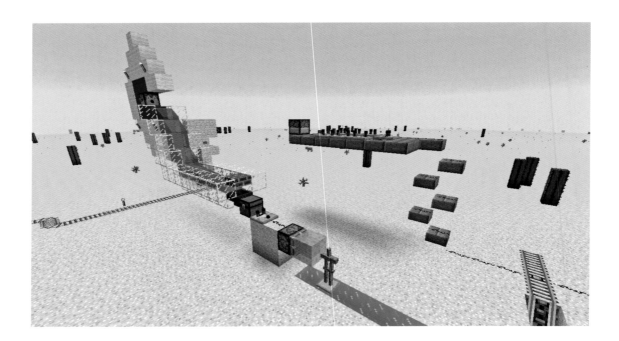

In this lab, you'll use simple mechanisms to create a chain reaction to accomplish a simple task, also known as Rube Goldberg machines. Consisting of mechanisms such as levers, pulleys, wheels and axles, screws, wedges, and gears, these machines are named after Rube Goldberg, a cartoonist and engineer who created famous newspaper cartoons. Some overly complex machines can take hours to build and seconds to perform. You'll get to build your own in and out of Minecraft.

FIND IT ONLINE

- Learn more about Rube Goldberg, his comic strips, contests, and more: www.rubegoldberg.com

In this activity, we're going to build a Rube Goldberg machine. We pulled together a bunch of items lying around to build our example. The materials list is just a suggestion; see what you have around your house.

■ APPROXIMATE TIME TO COMPLETE
1 hour

■ MATERIALS
Wooden train tracks with train
Dominoes
Large bouncy ball
Wood blocks
Books
Electrical surge protector with on/off switch
Electric fan

Fig. 1: Pull back on the ball to start the machine.

1. All great Rube Goldberg machines repurpose parts found around the house. While you design your machine, consider using old and new toys with string, tape, electrical switches, swinging bouncy balls, train tracks, balloons, and dominoes.

2. Every Rube Goldberg machine has a clever start. Try hanging a large bouncy ball taped on a string that will pendulum into something to kick-start your machine (fig. 1).

Fig. 2: This run has six reactions. Notice the small wood tree taped onto the power switch to make sure the fan turns on.

3. Our machine has six different reactions. A swinging ball hits the train that rolls into the dominoes. The dominoes hit the larger blocks, which hit the large wood train track pieces. The train track pieces fall onto the books, which tumble onto the electrical switch to turn on the fan (fig. 2).

4. It takes several tries to have one successful start-to-finish run (fig. 3). Don't worry if it takes dozens of attempts, as the best Rube Goldberg machines require a lot of patience.

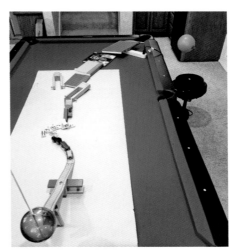

Fig. 3: It takes patience to devise a successful start-to-finish run.

WHAT'S THE SCIENCE?

Using his training as an engineer and his sense of humor, Rube Goldberg (1883-1970) created comically complex machines to accomplish simple tasks, such as using a napkin or a picking up soap that fell out of the bathtub. Rube Goldberg machines are a series of simple machines—lever, wheel and axle, pulley, inclined plane, wedge, and screw—which are the building blocks of more complex machines.

With a little creativity, you can use items in Minecraft to create reactions. Just as you built an actual machine in the family activity, you're going to design, build, test, and rebuild a Rube Goldberg machine in-game. You'll use dispensers, slime blocks, comparators, repeaters, pistons, detector rails, armor stands, and more!

- **Game mode**
  Creative

- **Approximate time to complete**
  90 minutes

1. Pick a fun location to craft your Rube Goldberg machine. Start and end your machine in a similar location. We've crafted a pumpkin pie delivery machine.

2. To start our Rube Goldberg chain reaction machine, we fire an arrow at a wooden button placed on the side of a dispenser. The dispenser releases a piece of redstone dust that flows down the river (fig. 1).

3. At the end of the river, the redstone enters the hopper. The hopper moves the redstone into the chest. Once the chest has the redstone, the redstone comparator is activated (fig. 2).

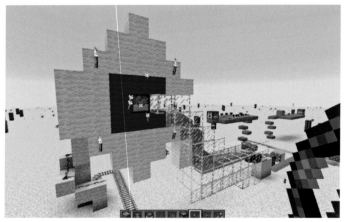

Fig. 1: Firing the arrow at the button causes the dispenser to release redstone dust that flows down the river and into the chest.

Fig. 2: Notice the half slab used to create an end to the river. Without the half slab, the water will flow out in all directions.

4. The redstone comparator sends a signal through redstone to activate the sticky piston. A slime block on the end of the sticky piston pushes the armor stand down the icy runway. The armor stand ends on a stone pressure plate (fig. 3).

5. The stone pressure plate sends a redstone signal to a powered redstone rail. Place a cart on top of the redstone rail. The block immediately behind the cart forces the cart to move once the redstone rail becomes powered (fig. 4).

6. The cart rides the rail to a detector rail that activates the redstone ladder. The signal burst up the ladder starts the redstone clock on top of the platform. The dispenser filled with arrows at the end of the redstone clock starts firing at the wooden button (fig. 5).

7. The last step is for the minecart with pumpkin pie in the chest to be delivered to the original firing station. The arrows from the dispenser activate the redstone rail and send the cart on its way.

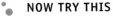

NOW TRY THIS

Search for Rube Goldberg in the app store on your mobile device for more Rube Goldberg machine fun.

Fig. 3: Hoppers are clever items. In this build, we're using a hopper to transfer the redstone dust collected from the end of the river into the chest.

Fig. 4: Be sure to add the block behind the minecart. Customize your build by adding or removing rail.

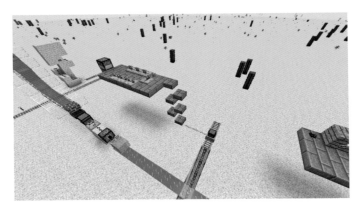

Fig. 5: The redstone ladder is a compact method for sending a signal vertically. Check out Lab 3 (page 36) for directions on how to build a redstone ladder.

You'll be diving into astronomy in this lab, where the challenge is to make a mini solar system in Minecraft. You'll park the planets in the sky right outside your science lab and create a beautiful nighttime view. In the family activity, you will focus on the ringed planet Saturn and make a clay model of its interior.

WHAT'S THE SCIENCE?

Planets in the inner solar system are solid, with heavy metallic cores. In the early solar system, the intense heat vaporized gases like hydrogen and helium and left these planets with hard, rocky surfaces. Saturn, like the other three outer planets, is known as a gas giant. The early outer solar system was much cooler. Common gases like helium and hydrogen did not vaporize and, instead, formed large gas planets with super-hot cores.

Family Activity: Clay Saturn

In this lab, you will be creating a model of the planet Saturn out of clay.

■ **APPROXIMATE TIME TO COMPLETE**
1 hour

■ **MATERIALS**
5 blocks of modeling clay, about 4 ounces (113 g) each, in assorted colors
Rolling pin
10 toothpicks
Sharp knife (get help from adult)

1. Although Saturn is a gas planet, astronomers think its core may be solid. Roll half a block of clay into a ball (fig. 1).

2. Select another color of clay and roll about half of it out flat. Cover the core with this "liquid neon" layer (fig. 2). Repeat to add two more layers, helium and hydrogen (fig. 3).

3. To create the ring disk, roll out the final color into a flat circle. With a toothpick, cut a hole out of the center that's just slightly smaller than your planet (fig. 4). Insert the toothpicks around the equator (fig. 5) and lay the ring disk on top of the toothpicks, stretching the center as needed.

4. With a sharp knife and adult supervision, cut a quarter section out of the planet to expose its interior (fig. 6).

Fig. 1: We used black clay to form the solid core.

Fig. 2: Roll out the clay to make it easier to cover each layer. This is the liquid neon layer.

Fig. 3: Add two more layers; helium is pink and hydrogen is yellow in our model.

Fig. 4: Cut a hole in the center using a toothpick to make a ring disk.

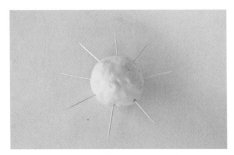
Fig. 5: Add toothpicks to support the ring disk.

Fig. 6: We added some leftover clay to our rings and cut out a section of the planet to reveal the gaseous core.

Gather the family and a few friends to help you create a solar system. In this lab, you'll use math to construct planetoids to enhance the sky view from your laboratory.

■ **GAME MODE**
Creative

■ **APPROXIMATE TIME TO COMPLETE**
1-2 hours

SKETCHNOTE CHALLENGE

Sketch your solar system and name each planet. Perhaps the names should relate to the material you used? Or named after ancient gods or superheroes? What would a planet named after Spider-Man look like? Astronomers sometimes use a memory trick to help them remember the order of the planets in our solar system: My Very Enthusiastic Mother Just Served Us Noodles (for Mercury, Venus, Earth, Mars, Jupiter, Saturn, Uranus, Neptune)! What might this look like if you drew it in your notebook?

Fig. 1: Build this frame in the directions *x, y,* and *z*. Each axis is 11 blocks of pink wool.

1. To build in the sky, you'll need to make a tall pillar that extends high into the air. Where you stop will be the base (or south pole) of your first planet. You likely already know about a number line. You might even have experience with graphing numbers using the coordinate system. It's the same system used in Minecraft to determine your location: *x, y,* and *z*.

2. Circles and spheres have a radius, which is the distance from the center to the outer edge. We'll make our first sphere with a radius of 5. Remember that number; it will come up again. Place your first block on the base (south pole of your planet) and then 10 more straight up for a total of 11 blocks. This will be the *y*-axis. Find the center and add 5 blocks on both sides. This is the *x*-axis. Finally, repeat this step from the center to create the *z*-axis (fig. 1).

Fig. 2: We used green wool to add an X shape at the end of each axis.

Fig. 3: Fill in the X shape, but leave each corner unfilled.

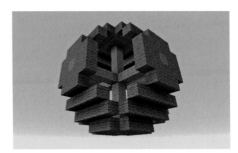

Fig. 4: Build 2 rows of 5 blocks (blue wool in image) on the south and north poles of your sphere.

3. At the end of each axis, create an X reaching outward from each end block by adding 2 blocks in all directions (fig. 2). Fill in each X to create a 5 × 5 square, but leave out each corner (fig. 3).

4. Beginning at the bottom, add 2 rows of 5 blocks each that climb like stairs upward. Repeat this step from the top downward (fig. 4).

5. Complete a similar task to step 3, but instead of rows, create 2 columns of 5 blocks. Add these columns all the way around the sphere (fig. 5).

6. Finally, add a few more blocks to fill in the remaining gaps and you'll end up with your first planet (fig. 6)!

7. Repeat this process and create as many planets as you would like. Experiment with different blocks, colors, and textures to create the ultimate solar system.

Fig. 5: Add 2 columns of 5 blocks (yellow wool in image) around your sphere from east to west.

Fig. 6: Almost done! Fill in the remaining holes with blocks (orange wool in image) and your planet is complete.

 NOW TRY THIS

- Construct a larger planet with a radius of 7 or 9. Is there a relationship between the radius and the number of rows and columns?
- Add a ring around a planet. Your ring should be at least three times the radius of the planet.
- Create a star like our Sun by using glowstone.

 FIND IT ONLINE

Want to create even more amazing shapes? Look no further than the Plotz website, a handy tool that helps you visualize Minecraft structures in 3D: *http://www.plotz.co.uk*

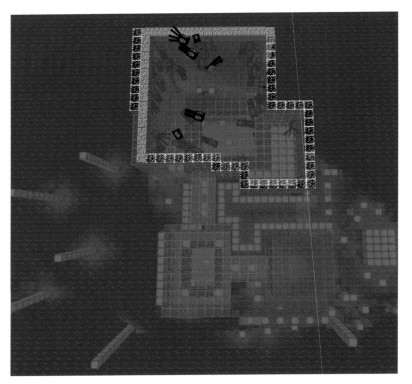

Put on your scuba gear! We're going to dive deep under the ocean and build an underwater oceanography station, a structure that will keep you safe, well fed, and investigating the bottom of the sea for hours. To begin, let's make a submarine and learn about the science of buoyancy.

This activity requires adult supervision and participation. You'll make a submarine out of plastic bottles (a great opportunity to recycle some empties), sink it, and then use your lung power to raise it once again.

■ **APPROXIMATE TIME TO COMPLETE**

30 minutes

■ **MATERIALS**

Small plastic or paper funnel
1 large (2L) plastic bottle
Sand, enough to fill most of the
  large bottle
Scissors
2 smaller (12oz) plastic bottles
4 rubber bands
2 drinking straws
Small amount of nonhardening
  modeling clay
2 binder clips
Ruler
Aquarium, water tank, or bathtub with
  water, and large enough to contain
  your model submarine

1. **Gather your materials. Using a funnel, fill the large plastic bottle with enough sand so that it gently sinks in the water. In our example, we filled the bottle two-thirds full (fig. 1).**

2. **With the scissors, poke a small hole in one side of the first small bottle. The hole needs to be large enough for a straw to enter. Find the opposite side of the small bottle and poke a larger hole, about twice the size of the first hole. Repeat with the second smaller bottle (fig. 2).**

3. Attach the small bottles (buoyancy tanks) on either side of the large bottle using the rubber bands. The small hole for each straw should be on top.Insert a straw into the hole in the top of each small bottle. Smear modeling clay around each straw to create a watertight seal. Attach a binder clip at the midpoint on each straw. This will be used to trap the air supply in each tank (fig. 3).

4. Place your submarine into the water. It should float as each buoyancy tank contains enough trapped gas to equalize forces.

5. Release each binder clip. The gas trapped inside each tank will escape through the straw and water will enter the larger hole underneath. The forces are no longer equal and your submarine sinks (fig. 4).

6. Now try to raise it from the bottom. Blow into both straws at the same time to force the water out and the carbon dioxide back into each tank. The submarine will rise as each tank fills with the less dense gas.

Fig. 1: Fill the large bottle with enough sand to gently sink it.

Fig. 2: The holes in the small bottles should be large enough to thread a straw through.

Fig. 3: Attach the smaller bottles, insert the straws, cover the area around each with modeling clay, and attach a binder clip at the midpoint of each.

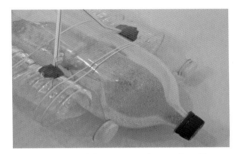

Fig. 4: Place sub in water, release the clips, and watch it sink as the air is replaced by water. To raise the sub, blow into both straws at the same time to force out water.

WHAT'S THE SCIENCE?

In terms a scientist would use, when the upward force of buoyancy is equal to the downward force of gravity, an object floats. To sink (submerge) your submarine, you let water into the outside tanks through the large hole in each, then gravity took over. To raise your submarine, you forced air into the tanks through the straw, forcing the water out. The upward force overcame the downward force.

Your challenge is to take what you've learned in this book and apply it to an underwater oceanography field station. You'll need your automation skills, command block knowledge, and a solid understanding of redstone mechanisms to make it work.

Lay out your field station on paper, first. It should include the following:

- Access to food and shelter
- A power supply
- Automated doors or a mob trap
- A teleport station to return to the surface hub
- A large fish tank and viewing platform

■ **GAME MODE**
Creative

■ **APPROXIMATE TIME TO COMPLETE**
3–4 hours

GO BEYOND

Dive into one of the world's great aquariums, Monterey Bay Aquarium, in Monterey, California. View online exhibits and fun activities:
https://goo.gl/iJRmYJ

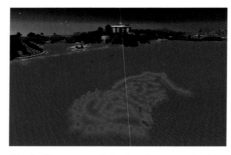

Fig. 1: Give yourself plenty of room to build. Light up the area with glowstone. Replace it with sea lanterns as you build.

Fig. 2: Build a small room, first. Add a door to create an air pocket, then right-click with a sponge to soak up all the water. You can then destroy the wet sponge.

1. **Working underwater can be a difficult challenge. You can't see very well, you move more slowly, and you need to remove lots of water as you build. Find a location that isn't too deep and is mostly flat. Lay out a large number of glowstone or sea lantern blocks to light your work area (fig. 1).**

2. **To get the hang of building underwater, let's start with a small section of your field station. In our model, we started with the bedroom that has the dimensions of 6 × 7. Lay down the floor and put up the walls and the roof. Place a door. The door creates an air pocket, even if it is left open. With the door closed, place a sponge in your hand and right-click. The sponge will absorb all the water in the room, leaving you with a wet sponge and a dry bedroom (fig. 2).**

3. **As you complete each building, surround it with a layer of glass, clear or colored. Now you can punch out windows anywhere without being flooded and it stops water drops from leaking through your roofed areas (fig. 3).**

4. **Connect separate builds with long corridors. Use lots of light and glass. Soak up the water as described in step 2 (fig. 4).**

5. **Build a room that has a great view of the ocean beyond and turn it into a giant aquarium by surrounding it with glass walls, several blocks away from your building (fig. 5). Place items on the sea floor that might be found in an aquarium and spawn squid when finished.**

6. **Finish by adding a teleport station, redstone-powered piston doors, and a power supply (fig. 6).**

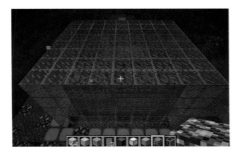

Fig. 3: Add glass all around to allow for instant window creation. It also stops the roof from leaking.

Fig. 4: Use corridors to connect each building in your complex.

SKETCHNOTE CHALLENGE

Lay out your design for the oceanography lab in your science journal. Label each part of the station. What might you build as additions in the future?

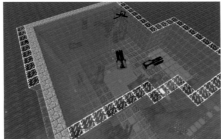

Fig. 5: Enclose an area around one of your larger buildings and turn it into an aquarium. Spawn squid and build items you might find in an aquarium.

Fig. 6: Add as many extras as you need to complete the challenge. You'll need a way back to land.

 NOW TRY THIS

- How else could you use command blocks in this build? Experiment with the /summon command in your aquarium.
- Every oceanographer needs a submarine. Build one and attach it to the lab by creating a docking station.

FIND IT ONLINE

Looking for some truly crazy things to incorporate into you undersea lab? Check out UnspeakableGaming's 20-minute video full of redstone ideas: *https://goo.gl/rd6JdE*

Extras

Opposite: Dot programming sheet for
Lab 21 Code Your Commands (see page 118).
Photocopy, scan and print, or download
at www.quartoknows.com/page/minecraft-stem.

Glossary

Activator Rail—When a minecart passes over an activator rail, a command is issued that will affect the minecart or the contents of the minecart.

Beacon—Beacons produce an extremely bright light source that can be seen from a great distance. They can also affect the status of a player who gets close to them.

Bedrock—Everyone loves digging in Minecraft, but eventually you'll hit bottom. Bedrock is the bottom layer and you cannot break this block in survival mode.

Biome—Every Minecraft world has multiple biomes or ecological regions. Fly around enough in creative mode and you will come across deserts, mountain ranges, oceans, jungles, plains, and many others.

Button—When activated, a button will release a short burst of power, enabling such actions as opening doors or powering other mechanisms.

Command Block—A special game block that enables custom commands to be issued within the game. Command blocks need to be activated by a redstone power source.

Comparator—When placed in redstone circuits, comparators compare adjacent signals within the circuit and act to maintain or turn off the signal. They can be used to subtract signal strength.

Compass—Compasses point players back to the spawn (starting) point.

Crafting Table—Players use a crafting table to craft, or create, artifacts used in the game.

Daylight Sensor—These blocks measure the output of light in the game and issue a redstone signal.

Detector Rail—These rails detect minecarts traveling over them and issue a redstone signal.

Dispenser—When activated, these blocks dispense items stored in them to players standing in front of the block.

Dropper—Like a dispenser, these blocks eject items stored in them. Unlike a dispenser, these blocks can be chained together and push items over a distance.

Dyes—Obtained by collecting flowers or mineral ores, dyes are useful in creating different colored fireworks.

Elytra—Wing-like item that enables players to glide and fly.

Lever—Levers open or close redstone circuits.

Mechanisms—Component blocks and devices in the game that allow actions to be undertaken. Piston doors are an example of a mechanism.

Mods—The creative team behind Minecraft has opened the game up to other developers by allowing them to create modifications (mods) to the original game. These modifications are mostly free and change the game by adding new features or modifying existing ones.

Note Block—Assorted musical notes can be played through note blocks when they are activated by redstone.

Observer Block—These blocks monitor the state of blocks placed next to them and issue a redstone signal when a change in condition is observed.

Piston—There are two kinds of pistons in Minecraft. Both push blocks in the direction the piston is facing. When using sticky pistons, many of the pushed blocks stick to the piston, which enables the block to be pulled back.

Powered Rail—Used in combination with a power source, these rails will move a minecart in any desired direction.

Pressure Plate—When used as a redstone component, these nonsolid blocks activate a mechanism when stepped upon.

Redstone—A special block in Minecraft that releases dust when broken and can be used to provide power to crafted items like pistons and automated doors.

Redstone Lamp—Blocks that emit a light source when activated by a redstone source.

Redstone Torch—A miniature and portable power source used to activate redstone devices.

Repeater—A block that can be used to extend the length of a redstone signal or delay it. Repeaters may also be used to lock a signal into one state or prevent signals from moving backward.

Spawn—This is the location where everyone will initially arrive in a new world. Your spawn point changes once you create a home with a bed and lay in it. When you die in survival mode, you will respawn at this point.

Trapped Chest—Like a regular Minecraft chest, this chest can store items. Unlike a regular chest, this chest can be filled remotely or be used to dispense an item with a command block.

Trip Wire—Trip wires are used to detect objects like players or minecarts passing through them. They will then activate a redstone circuit and any associated mechanisms.

LAB NUMBER AND TITLE	FEATURED STEM CONCEPT(S)	NGSS (Next Generation Science Standards) www.nextgenscience.org	INTERNATIONAL BACCALAUREATE www.ibo.org
1 Redstone Laboratory	Electrical engineering, photovoltaic sensors, solar astronomy, programming, note and pitch	3-PS2-3 Motion and Stability: Forces and Interactions	Physics: D.1 Stellar Quantities, 8.1 Energy Sources
2 All Aboard	Inertia, kinetic and potential energy, velocity	MS-PS2-2 Motion and Stability: Forces and Interactions	Physics: 2.3 Work, Energy and Power, 2.4 Momentum and Impulse
3 Gravity Impact	Kinetic energy, energy transference	4-ESS2-1 Earth's Systems	Physics: 2.3 Work, Energy and Power, 6.2 Newton's Law of Gravitation
4 Piston Power	Pascal's principle, density and pressure	Matter and Its Interactions	Physics: Option B.3 Fluid and Fluid Dynamics
5 Map Maker	Geography and technology	MS-ESS2-6 Earth's Systems	MYP: Individuals and Societies
6 Let There Be Light	Exothermic and endothermic reactions, chemistry, electromagnetic spectrum	HS. Waves and Electromagnetic Radiation	Physics: 2.4 Momentum and Impulse; Chemistry: 15.2 Entropy and Spontaneity
7 Crystals	Thermal energy, exothermic reactions	5. Earth's Systems	Physics: 3.1 Thermal Concepts
8 Catch a Wave	Wave Energy	PS4 Waves and Their Applications in Technologies for Information Transfer	Physics: 4.2 Traveling Waves, 4.3 Wave Characteristics, 4.4 Wave Behavior
9 Mars Space Station	Engineering	Space Systems	Engineering Physics: Option B.14 Engineering Physics; Physics: D.1 Stellar Quantities
10 Zipline	Air resistance, friction	Forces and Interactions: Pushes and Pulls	Physics: 2.1 Motion
11 Weather Watcher	Meteorology	Weather and Climate	MYP: Individuals and Societies
12 Explosions Everywhere!	Chemistry, algebra, electrical engineering, mineralogy	Endothermic/Exothermic	Physics: 2.4 Momentum and Impulse; Chemistry: 15.2 Entropy and Spontaneity

LAB NUMBER AND TITLE	FEATURED STEM CONCEPT(S)	NGSS (Next Generation Science Standards) www.nextgenscience.org	INTERNATIONAL BACCALAUREATE www.ibo.org
13 Layers of the Earth	Geology, soil science	4-ESS2-1 Earth's Systems	Biology: Topic 4 Ecology
14 Iron Age	Magnetism	HS-PS2-5 Motion and Stability: Forces and Interactions	Physics: 11.1 Electromagnetic Induction, 5.4 Magnetic Effects of Electric Currents, 7.1 Discrete Energy and Radioactivity; Chemistry: 12.1 Electrons in Atoms
15 Volcanic Activity	Volcanism, geology, chemistry, force and motion	5. Earth's Systems	Biology: Topic 4 Ecology; Physics: 2.4 Momentum and Impulse
16 Land of the Giants	Paleontology and archaeology	MS-ESS2-3 Earth's Systems	Biology: 4.1 Species, Community and Ecosystem, 5.1 Fossil Record
17 Egg Farm	Agriculture, engineering, programming	5-ESS3 Earth and Human Activity	Biology: 5.3 Classification of Biodiversity
18 Build a Battery	Chemical energy, electrical energy	MS. Energy	Physics: 5.3 Electric Cells
19 Create an Ecosystem	Horticulture	HS-LS2-5 Ecosystems: Interactions, Energy, and Dynamics	Physics 3.1 Thermal Concepts; Biology: 2.2 Water, 4.1 Nutrient Cycling
20 Quantum Physics	Polarization, coding	HS-PS4 Waves and Their Applications in Technologies for Information Transfer	Physics: Topic 12 Quantum and Nuclear Physics
21 Code Your Commands	Technology, coding	ISTE student standards	ISTE student standards
22 Chain Reaction Contraption	Simple machines	3-PS2 Motion and Stability: Forces and Interactions	Physics: 2.2 Forces
23 Pocket Solar System	Astronomy, geology, geometry	HS. Space Systems	Physics: 1.1 Measurements in Physics, D.1 Stellar Quantities
24 Under the Sea	Buoyancy, ecosystem	MS-LS2-5 Ecosystems: Interactions, Energy, and Dynamics	Biology: Option C Species and Communities, Communities and Ecosystems

Resources

Adam Clarke
www.thecommonpeople.tv

Altitude
https://goo.gl/8A1VmN

Anaglyphs of Mars
https://goo.gl/8C4JWm

Battery
https://goo.gl/ez1fQ

Chicken Egg Collector
https://goo.gl/TiJvFe

Cloud Matching Game
https://goo.gl/noXRhj

Color Vision
https://goo.gl/RBEHOh

Command Block
https://goo.gl/LryCxv

Commands
https://goo.gl/UKwyRP

Commands and Cheats
https://goo.gl/hYMgjn

Cooked Chicken Farm
https://goo.gl/apD1Fi

Coordinates of a Block
https://goo.gl/TL7tk1

Crystals in Mineral Water
https://goo.gl/UbzCuc

Dragnoz
www.dragnoz.com

Ferro Fluid
https://goo.gl/qCyjwH

Find Fossils
https://goo.gl/Qyw1YW

Firework Rocket
https://goo.gl/SzMvLV

Fossils
https://goo.gl/JFua7Z

Games and Activities:
Monterey Bay Aquarium
https://goo.gl/iJRmYJ

Ice Wheel Bike by Colin Furze
https://goo.gl/n9QE41

Immersive Minds
www.immersiveminds.com

Jiwi's Machines
http://jiwismachines.com

Jragon—Learn How to Make Minecraft
Commands's Youtube Channel
https://goo.gl/zl67WA

Kundt's tube
https://goo.gl/cMJqKw

Marble Roller Coaster
https://goo.gl/hgX7E6

Mars for Kids: NASA
https://goo.gl/zWHpJf

Mine Gage
www.minegage.com

Minecraft Realm's Fireworks
and Freeform Forts
https://goo.gl/2Sjb96

Minecraft Shapes
www.plotz.co.uk

National Geographic Kids
https://goo.gl/6T4TiL

Note Block
https://goo.gl/P6ewO6

Prism
https://goo.gl/BAOq7o

Rainbow Beacon
https://goo.gl/HeaeDz

Rainbow Illustration
https://goo.gl/4pj2tt

Redstone Creations
https://goo.gl/x0O7op

Redstone Doors and Trapdoors
https://goo.gl/F1Xx5w

Redstone Tutorials
https://goo.gl/rrJydV

About the Authors

Rube Goldberg
www.rubegoldberg.com

Science Friday
https://goo.gl/wkw4oy

STMD Centennial Challenges: NASA
https://goo.gl/FY2V4s

Terraria
https://terraria.org

Tour of the Moon by NASA Goddard
https://goo.gl/X2u2w

Underwater Redstone House
https://goo.gl/rd6JdE

Vacuum Chamber by BBC
https://goo.gl/mXojgZ

Working Dam
https://goo.gl/PGM31K

World Edit Tips and Tricks
https://goo.gl/hXF1UX

JOHN MILLER has been a middle school teacher in King City, California, for the past 24 years and has experience teaching grades 6 through 8 in every content area. He holds both multiple- and single- subject credentials, and his interests include astronomy, anthropology, and world history. John earned an MA in Educational Technology and loves to dive deep into instructional design. He has been recognized as Teacher of the Year for Monterey County and has been honored as a finalist for California State Teacher of the Year. In addition to being a CUE Lead Learner and Minecraft Global Mentor and Trainer, he is a Google Innovator and coauthor of *Unofficial Minecraft Lab for Kids* (Quarry Books) and a contributing author of *Minecraft in the Classroom* (Peachpit Press). John spends his free time rock climbing and traveling the world with his talented wife and educator, Audrey. You can learn more about John and contact him by visiting his blog, Minecraft.edtecworks.com.

CHRIS FORNELL SCOTT is the founder and executive director of Woven Learning and Technology, a California nonprofit that runs Minecrafter Camps. One of his life goals is to inspire kids to dream big. In 2016, he moved onto a sailboat with his wife, three boys, and a beagle. You can find out more about Chris and his family at www.secretwateradventure.com.

Index

Also Available

Unofficial Minecraft Lab for Kids
978-1-63159-117-4

Math Lab for Kids
978-1-63159-252-2

Kitchen Science Lab for Kids
978-1-59253-925-3

Outdoor Science Lab for Kids
978-1-63159-115-0